THE SECRETS OF ECONOMIC AND INDUSTRIAL ESPIONAGE

DR. NASSER AFIFY

2018

Table of Contents

INTRODUCTION…………………………………………	1
1- DEFINTION OF ECONOMIC AND INDUSTRIAL ESPIONAGE…………………………………….……	3
2- HISTORY OF ECONOMIC AND INDUSTRIAL ESPIONAGE…………………………………………	9
3- THE ROLE OF TECHNOLOGY IN EXTENTION OF ECONOMIC ESPIONAGE………………………	38
4- SOURCES OF RISK AND THREAT…………………	57
5- THE ECONOMIC ESPIONAGE ACT (EEA) OF 1996…………………………………………………………	76
6- THE PROTECTION FROM ECONOMIC ESPIONAGE………………………………………………	85
7- THE ROLE OF CHINA IN ECONOMIC ESPIONAGE………………………………………………	93
8- LAWS OF CYBER WORLD……………………………	112
CONCLUSION………………………………………………	128
REFERENCES……………………………………………...	139

INTRODUCTION

Since the end of the Cold War industrial intelligence has become a critical area of interest to governments as well as non-state actors engaged in the global competition over new innovations and technologies. Especially in Europe, where production can no longer compete with rising powers such as China, the main thrust in the economic sector has been towards research and development. It can thus be said that the rise of information technology in both civilian and military use has maximized the resources allocated to discovering new trends and inventions by clandestine means while protecting intellectual capital and sensitive information has become instrumental for the corporate security of private sector actors and a first priority for national intelligence agencies.

Industrial intelligence in the post-Cold War era during the last two decades the global economy has developed at an ever increasing speed. The economy affects political and military relations and many other aspects of life.

Globalization has resulted in new conditions for international economy that demand a modern understanding of the definition of loyalty to nation states. This trend together with the dual use of technologies, meaning both civilian and military use, guarantees that industrial intelligence will continue to gain importance while the differences in defense and industrial applications become more unclear.

The phenomenon of globalization coupled with the explosion of information technology has had a huge impact on the way societies and nations function. The post-Cold War period has also brought new secret information demands to the fore. Technological advances with enormous economic and military potential generate intensive competition on patents, markets and technological superiority. Interests related to security, technology and the economy are often connected. When assessing the intelligence threat on the economic and technological areas, traditional considerations such as military-strategic importance and geopolitical situation are less relevant. Other aspects, such as a country's international status in research, industry and export become more important. Economic and social strengths may be viewed as the future primary factors of world influence. The national securities of nations are threatened by the failure to adapt our thinking with the ongoing changes in the world around us.

1. DEFINITION OF ECONOMIC AND INDUSTRIAL ESPIONAGE

Espionage, in general, is the practice of spying or using spies to obtain information about the plans and activities especially of a foreign government or a competing company.

It is the practice of spying or of using spies, typically by governments to obtain political and military information. And it is the activity of finding out the political, military, or industrial secrets of your enemies or rivals by using spies. It is also the act of organized spying, usually with the goal of uncovering sensitive military or political information. I may be defined as attempts to discover your enemy's political, military, or industrial secrets using secret methods. Someone who does this is a spy.

Espionage also is the discovering of secrets, especially political or military information of another country or the industrial information of a business.

Economic espionage may be defined as the unlawful targeting and theft of a nation's critical economic intelligence. Economic espionage may include the clandestine acquisition or outright theft of invaluable proprietary information in a number of areas including technology, finance and government policy. Economic espionage differs from corporate or industrial espionage in a number of ways – it is likely to be state-sponsored, have motives other than profit or gain (such as closing a technology gap) and be much larger in scale and scope.

It is the unlawful or clandestine targeting or acquisition of sensitive financial, trade or economic policy information; proprietary economic information; or technological information.

In USA It is foreign power-sponsored or coordinated intelligence activity directed at the U.S. government or U.S. corporations, establishments, or persons, designed to unlawfully or clandestinely influence sensitive economic policy decisions or to unlawfully obtain sensitive financial, trade, or economic policy information; proprietary economic information; or critical technologies. This theft, through open and clandestine methods, can provide foreign entities with vital proprietary economic information at a fraction of the true cost of its research and development, causing significant economic losses.

It is also the knowing misappropriation of trade secrets with the knowledge or intent that the offense will benefit a foreign government, foreign instrumentality, or foreign agent. Misappropriation includes, but is not limited to, stealing, copying, altering, destroying, transmitting, sending, receiving, buying, possessing, or conspiring to obtain trade secrets without authorization. And it is attempting to obtain trade secrets by dishonest means, as by telephone or computer-tapping, infiltration of a competitor's workforce.

Economic espionage is a complex legal definition that involves the theft of trade secrets. In effect, economic espionage is the use of a stolen trade secret to benefit foreign powers or in commercial or economic trade. Ideas, formulas or products can all be trade secrets. Those who commit economic espionage do so in order to gain and benefit from proprietary information developed by businesses. It is estimated that economic espionage has caused business losses in the trillions of dollars over the last decade alone.

Economic espionage is prohibited by the Economic Espionage Act of 1996 (18 U.S.C. § 1831-1839). Section 1831 of the Act criminalizes the theft and use of stolen trade secrets to benefit foreign powers, while Section 1832 makes illegal the theft of such trade secrets for commercial or economic gain. This includes the duplication or copying of a trade secret with the intention to economically benefit from it and/or the conspiracy to do so.

The penalties for economic espionage can be stiff – those using stolen trade secrets to benefit a foreign government face a fine of up to $500,000 and/or up to 15 years in federal prison, while those who steal trade secrets for their own gain may be fined or put in prison for up to ten years. Companies that engage in economic espionage also face harsh consequences – they can be fined up to $10 million for stealing trade secrets for another government and up to $5 million for using stolen secrets for their own gain.

In addition to prosecution in the United States, the Economic Espionage Act also applies to perpetrators who victimize U.S. citizens, affect the United States in a substantial form, or are a U.S. citizen themselves. The U.S.

Department of Justice prosecutes economic espionage with assistance from the CIA and other international bodies.

Industrial espionage is the covert and sometimes illegal practice of investigating competitors to gain a business advantage. The target of investigation might be a trade secret such as a proprietary product specification or formula, or information about business plans. In many cases, industrial spies are simply seeking any data that their organization can exploit to its advantage.

An industrial spy may be an insider threat, such as an individual who has gained employment with the company with the purpose of spying or a disgruntled employee who trades information for personal gain or revenge. Spies may also infiltrate through social engineering tactics, for example by tricking an employee into divulging privileged information.

Spies sometimes physically breach the target organization and investigate the premises. In that case, a spy might search waste baskets or copy files or hard drives of unattended computers. Increasingly, the intrusion is through the corporate network. Typically, a targeted attack is conducted to gain initial network access and then an advanced persistent threat (APT) is carried out for continued data theft. The capacity of cell phones to record and transmit can also be exploited by leaving a phone in a boardroom, for example, and monitoring a meeting remotely. Recording devices are also secreted in a variety of items including eyeglasses, pens and USB sticks.

Industrial espionage is distinct from competitive intelligence (CI), which is confined to the gathering of publicly available information.

2. HISTORY OF ECONOMIC AND INDUSTRIAL ESPIONAGE

Throughout history, industrial espionage has remained a pervasive channel for technology transfer. Possibly the earliest recorded incidence of state-sponsored industrial espionage occurred in the 6th century AD, when two Nestorian monks successfully smuggled silkworm eggs, likely hidden in bamboo canes, from China into the Byzantine Empire .

This daring feat, an important juncture in the economic history of the Early Middle Ages, led to the breaking of two monopolies: that of Chinese silk production and that of the Persian silk trade with the West. As a result, Byzantine silk became one of the Empire's most profitable commodities while also providing a valuable medium of exchange, and several cities developed into major textile centers as a result.

In the late eighteenth and early nineteenth centuries, "the United States emerged as the world's industrial leader by illicitly appropriating mechanical and scientific innovations from Europe" as "American industrial spies roamed the British Isles, seeking not just new machines but skilled workers who could run and maintain those machines".

The use of spies to steal intelligence from competitors is not a new phenomenon; it began with the development of the global market and international trade and can be found all throughout history. For example, Bergier writes that as early as mid-6 th century AD, a princess traveled to China and placed silk worms in her flowered hat. She then brought them back to Europe in order to understand how silk was produced. Another early secret before the industrialization of society was how to master flints.

The Cretans held this technology and spies were sent to gain knowledge on this delicate process. It was not until the industrial revolution that the involvement in trade secret theft offered more than just knowledge on how to produce goods. During the 18th and 19th century and the industrial revolution, China was the first nation to discover and mass produce porcelain. Because of porcelain's potential for wealth, many nations sent spies to steal the manufacturing process from China. France was the first successful nation in doing so.

From that point forward, many nations were also successful in gaining access to the manufacturing process of porcelain. Other highly sought after information included: rocket technology, hermetic sealing, gunpowder, acids, and food preservation, the manufacturing of gold, antimony, steel, cold light, and purification of diamonds. From the late 1800s through the early 1900s, military espionage began to move to the forefront.

This military intelligence was centered on technologies that could help countries win war battles. Specifically during World War I and World War II, spies were relied on heavily to gain a military advantage. The most highly sought after information during this time period was: poison gas, explosive missiles, ammunition technologies, submarine technologies, rust proof steel, cannons, and atom bomb technologies. Although war technologies proved vital to spies during war times, once the war came to an end, the return to industrial espionage took place.

Economic espionage and trade secret theft is not a new phenomenon. For example, it has been used since the invention of the wheel and throughout pre-industrial society. Also, secrets for wheel making were stolen from the Roman Empire by the Celts, and simple techniques for making silk products were stolen from the Chinese by the Italians.

Not all acts of theft are needed to be so covert. Most acts of espionage are committed though simple activities, such as over-hearing a conversation, or observing a document in legal open spaces. In fact, in some instances of economic espionage and in some nations, competitors wanting to gain access to trade secrets would visit factories and shipyards to observe and steal manufacturing techniques.

Throughout history, a common method used to misappropriate trade secrets is the MICES (money, ideology, compromise, ego, and sexual entrapment) technique. MICES is used to encourage individuals to steal trade secrets due to an alliance with a foreign nation, or different beliefs than those of the employer.

The United States also frequently engages in economic espionage. During the 1800s, the United States successfully stole trade secrets from Great Britain to increase prosperity of the American textile industry. Francis Cabot Lowell traveled to Britain to spy on Britain's textile industry and steal water-driving cotton-weaving technology. Throughout history, the prevalence, sophistication, and value of losses have steadily increased due to MICES.

Industrial society is at an even greater risk of economic espionage. Due to the increase in technology, globalization, and the need for economic dominance, economic espionage is steadily increasing. Because of these increases, economic espionage "is the front line of a new world economic war". Prior to the Cold War, the focus was on protecting military intelligence but has now shifted towards United States' corporations.

In the post war era of today's society, there is no longer a need for the use of "war spies" in order to gain access to military secrets. The attention, therefore, has shifted towards becoming the leading nation in the international economic competition. As the Cold War came to an end, the "war spies" needed new employment. These old time spies of the Cold War did not just simply disappear. Many of them became employed by companies as corporate spies. They often become privatized and, "inaugurated Cold War II, the era of the global surveillance economy".

With the increase in technology, globalization, and the need for economic dominance, companies have new, more sophisticated methods of obtaining intellectual property. It is estimated that of the 173 nations worldwide, nearly 57 are actively seeking to steal trade secrets from the United States' corporations. However, the United States is not the only targeted nation for trade secrets. Many other nations, such as China, Japan, and Israel, whose corporations hold value in the world market, are often victimized, too. This worldwide problem lead to the creation of the Economic Espionage Act of 1996.

There are many ways in which a company or organization, can classify intellectual property in order to help safeguard information from becoming compromised. Patents, copyrights, trademarks, and trade secrets are all used to classify intellectual property.

These can be used in combination or in part, to better protect information from the criminal act of economic espionage. First, patents are used to promote two objectives: to show product designs and to control the global market on the established product. Patents allow consumers to see product designs and goals of technological goods which promote investment and allow for the products to be sold at the lowest possible price.

Patents protect the producer from a competitor building an identical product, therefore, reducing the likelihood of a competitive market. That is, no one else can produce the product with the same specifications unless the patent is revoked or removed. This allows for companies to keep costs low, as they do not have to compete for profits on a specific good. Within the application process for a patent, a company must provide and explain all details related to the product and its design.

These records are then published publically and easily accessible for viewing by all, including corporate spies. During this process, a company must make sure the benefits of ensuring a patent outweigh the possible risks. Secondly, information classified under copyright is strictly related to all forms of expression. A copyright simply protects written forms of expression, not ideas. At the initial installment of these laws, copyright proof laws were only directed at protecting written books, maps, and charts. It has most recently been expanded to include any and all forms of expression such as, novels, motion pictures, music, instruction manuals, bookkeeping forms, and computer programs.

There is, however, one major lacking component under copyright law; it does not protect ideas. Copyrights differ from patents in the essence that copyrights protect expressions, such as written materials, while patents protect products from being identically manufactured by a competitor. Thirdly, trademarks are used to legally protect brands and its products from competitors who attempt to mock an original product.

Basically, a trademark is a word, symbol, or name used to identify the source of the product. Historically, trademarks were used to protect the consumer against market confusion pertaining to where the consumer good originated. In modern society, trademark law, "is to give legal force to the practice of brand extension, giving trademark owners' rights not only in the markets where their brands first acquired fame, but in other markets as well".

This allows for a company like Coca-Cola to retain its name worldwide in multiple global markets without having multiple companies with similar names trying to replicate the actual trademarked brand of Coca-Cola.

Lastly, trade secrets are the most common way in which companies classify their intellectual information in order to protect intellectual ideas. This is an important breakthrough because intellectual property law withholds protection from ideas. Previously, a person's ideas were not protected against theft. Trade secrets allow for a person's or company's ideas to be protected from being stolen without any form of consent. Trade secrets are the most all inclusive way to protect intellectual property.

Through the use of trade secrets, companies can better safeguard their intellectual property. It should be noted, however, that in order for trade secret law to be enforced, the victimized entity must have engaged in reasonable actions to maintain secrecy.

Economic espionage has been around ever since nation states have existed and since there has been competition between nations and companies. The ancient Egyptians ran an intelligence service developed to gain information about their rivals, the Chinese attempted to protect the secret of porcelain, the method of production was, however, discovered by a French Jesuit and so reached Europe.

Today nations and companies spend a huge amount of money every year on trying to discover secrets their competitors attempt to protect. The overall economic cost of espionage cannot be calculated as the budgets for Intelligence Agencies who are the main practitioners of economic espionage, are a closely guarded secret.

It is however known, that the Chinese Intelligence Services employ over one million people to both protect the country from within and unearth the secrets of others. The economic damage caused by the loss of information is also unquantifiable. The FBI estimates that economic espionage costs the US around 100 Billion $ per year, the German Ministry of the Interior estimates the damage to Germany at around 20 Billion EURO. Industrial Espionage, unlike Economic espionage, is conducted by private companies.

Aims and methods are similar; however government agencies have the advantage of being able to employ highly sophisticated technical means in order to gather information. Increasingly however, private organizations working for the private sector are using equipment and methods which only a few years ago would only have been used by intelligence agencies.

The rapid increase in cyber-attacks on companies is also due to the fact that unscrupulous "consultants" are now also using electronic means to gather confidential information, or are seeking to disrupt the systems of the competition in order to gain an advantage for their clients. Such cyber-attacks on businesses can be expected to increase.

Companies are quite rightly investing significant sums of money in order to ensure that their EDP systems are as robust as possible in order to protect confidential information. The weakest link is however the employee and not the hard and soft ware. Security does not begin and end in the computer department, it is an issue which affects all departments within a company and is a top management issue. The firewalls and CCTV systems can be state of the art, if however an employee is willing to pass on confidential information or reveal passwords, the best wall can be broached with relative ease.

Shady consultants and foreign agents are well schooled in the art of social engineering. This process, which can take time, is designed to ensure that a target is sufficiently manipulated to reveal the secrets of a company. This can take the form of creating friendship, usually by providing a life style the victim could otherwise not afford. In the first instance information of little real value is asked for, gradually the stakes are raised until the informant is so deep into the role of informant that he cannot escape. At this point the real information the agent is seeing is requested, accompanied by the threat of revealing what has taken place should the information not be handed over. Most persons in such a position hand over the information.

The outcome for the informant is not very bright. If the person is a low level employee, recruited to get hold of one specific piece of information, they will be discarded. Only sources at a decision making position might be retained and further induced to reveal information. Open Source Intelligence (OSINT) is frequently used both to gather information on companies but also on people who might be targeted as a source.

There is a huge amount of information in the Web and in publications. This can be further refined by legal visits to companies, seminars, trade fairs and social gatherings. The latter has the advantage of combining both social engineering methods and the gathering of information. Whilst OSINT will not replace Human Intelligence (HUMINT), the rapid growth of freely available information and computer programs which allow analysts to rapidly sift through gigabytes of electronic information has increased the vulnerability of companies. The willingness of people to provide private information on such sites as Facebook is alarming as it offers those who seek to target weak links in companies an easy way to identify likely candidates.

A recent penetration test in the US gives a good example of how OSINT and HUMINT methods can result in the loss of information. A High-Tec company asked a security consultant to test the defenses the company had constructed to counter the loss of information. The consultants, using OSINT methods, managed to place a part time employee in the company using a false name and a fictitious background.

By using social engineering skills this person was able to gain access to top secret information relating to the configuration of the fire wall and also to pass words. This information was passed on to external hackers who were able to gather sensitive information which, if it had been passed on to competitors, would have resulted in a loss to the company of around 1 Billion$. The company had built up a robust defense from attacks from outside; it had simply forgotten that the enemy can also come from within. Given that many companies are networked and expect their senior management to be electronically reachable at all times, the dangers of losing information are greater outside the office rather than within.

The use of hand held devices or lap top computers when on a business trip represent a major threat to the security of data. Computers or other electronic devices left in bed rooms or in meeting rooms can be compromised and land line calls as well as calls on mobile phones intercepted. Such threats are barely recognized and many executives endanger their company by not sticking to simple precautions. One should simply assume that all information carried with one in electronic form can be accessed and should avoid if at all possible taking any such information on a business trip and leaving it unguarded.

A further threat is blackmail – many a piece of hot information has come out of entering into a compromising position far from the marriage bed. Some 45 % of all companies fall victim of some form of economic crime, according to international consultancy KPMG. Large companies report an average of incidences per year; many incidences remain unreported as companies do not want the general public to be aware of the problem.

Retailers, affected by numerous low value losses even factor the economic cost of theft into their pricing structure. IP theft and counterfeiting also show no sign of abating. The global trade in illicit goods is increasing: the number of counterfeits has grown at eight times the speed of legitimate trade according to Interpol, resulting in global commercial losses in the region of 500 Billion $, equal to around 7 % of world trade and is largely built around the same global complex distribution chains associated with legitimate trade flows.

Organized crime has built increasingly dense infrastructures to smuggle goods such as cigarettes, alcohol and drugs. Such groups are becoming increasingly sophisticated through international links, the use of legitimate business structures and violence. They will become increasingly entrenched through growing influence (via corruption) and their associated level of social and economic infiltration and integration. In some countries, such as Angola or Russia, organized crime can account for up to half the national economy.

These networks conduct criminal activities varying in structure, length and complexity, but most groups will continue to possess a core membership around which there is a cluster of subordinates, specialists and transient members with a network of dispensable associates or low level criminals used to carry out logistical and criminally related tasks. Such groups use a risk based approach to activities by threatening violence in the case of betrayal and by transferring risks to lower level criminals or using specialists on a need only basis.

As a result of the latter, we now have highly specialized criminal service organizations offering quality services in the field of IT, finance, forgery or logistics. Such specialists offer criminal organizations the possibility of cyber-attacks rather than old fashioned robbery and furthermore the possibility of using the Internet to launder the proceeds of their illegal activities.

Economic crime has both gone global and increasingly electronic. Many observers believe that the links between transnational organized crime and political violence will continue to grow. There have been or are numerous examples of armed groups resorting to smuggling to finance their violence: narcotics have been smuggled by the

Kosovo Liberation Army, the Kurdish workers Party, the Islamic Movement of Uzbekistan, the Taliban and the Irish Republican Army.

Thus organized crime will increasingly corrupt and undermine effective governance from the local to the state level and in some cases replace the legal government. The list of countries considered to be failed states or failing states is growing in Africa but also in Latin America, Asia and the Middle East. The problem of this development is more dangerous than is generally understood. The human security implications of state failure include armed conflict, famine, disease outbreaks, mass migration and an acceptance of organized crime.

Such an environment is hardly one companies would like to do business in, certainly not without taking robust measures to mitigate the associated risks involved.

Whilst globalization has acted as a facilitator of growth, it also serves to increase susceptibility to risk through interconnectedness between business, markets, people and nations.

At the same time, the pace of change has increased dramatically, meaning that the consequences of a risk event may become wider and more immediately felt by companies than previously envisioned. As threats manifest, they will have a widespread impact on business activities through the interplay of multiple factors. The loss of information to a competitor has an impact of the financial performance of a company and also is damaging to the reputation, which in turn can result in a declining share price. For the board of such a company the implications can be serious if it is shown that the company had not taken the necessary steps to protect the company from the loss of information.

Thus the loss of information becomes a compliance issue with all the consequences for those responsible at board level. An incidence of corruption within a company can in the same way damage the company financially and have compliance consequences for the board if it can be proven that due care to avoid such incidences had not been taken. It can furthermore result in companies who have tolerated corrupt practices from being barred from tendering for contracts in certain countries or for international organizations.

Siemens, for example, was not allowed to bid for a contract for a mass urban transportation system in San

Diego following the recent investigation into corrupt practices in relation to bribe paying in return for contracts. At the root of the problem is not an exogenous factor such as a pandemic or breakdown in infrastructure or even a natural disaster. Such risks are outside the control of companies and organizations can prepare for such an event in order to mitigate the impact on the company.

The main risk is the employee who, for whatever reason, is induced to act in a manner which is criminal and thus damages both the reputation of the company and causes economic damage. The enemy might be outside the company but the way into the company requires inside help. Companies can protect themselves from exogenous threats such as electronic monitoring, tapping of phone calls or from burglary by using technical means.

Such measures, however, do not protect companies from being exploited by employees. Senior executives or owners of companies are reluctant to believe that employees can be disloyal. In investigations of such cases one often hears that "we don't have that kind of problem". Alas, that is not the case and as in society any company also has its share of individuals prone to take rules and regulations lightly. Companies need to become aware of this and need to screen those in positions of responsibility closely prior to them joining the company.

Such pre-employment screening is commonplace in many Anglo Saxon companies, but in continental European countries screening is the exception rather than the rule. The monitoring of persons on a regular basis once they have joined the company is one fraught with problems in countries with high levels of personal data protection. However, controls need to be introduced in accordance with local laws in order to keep up the pressure on employees to perform to agreed guidelines.

Such measures also include job rotation in the purchasing departments in order to prevent the creation of corrupt networks or the practice of two or more employees signing off on contracts. At the same time companies need to screen their business partners on a regular basis in order to prevent the company from doing business with corrupt partners. Not all information can be protected, nor does it need to be. Companies therefore need to decide what information is confidential or secret and even top secret.

Confidential information is normally the kind of information all employees can share. If such information is leaked to competitors the consequences are not usually damaging. A leak of confidential information can however result in later damages to the company as it could reveal avenues for a future attack. Examples of this are internal phone lists which could allow a hacker to impersonate an employee in the computer department and thus gain access to valuable data in internal databases.

There need to be clear rules about the circulation and destruction of such information and these rules need to be enforced. Secret and top secret information needs to be protected by restricting access to those who really need to know and by the establishment of clear paper trails in order to easily identify possible leaks rapidly.

Rules on copying such information and on encryption need to be established. Any hard copy of such information needs be held in a secure place and shredded rather than disposed in locked containers for shredding by external service providers. It should be remembered that the easiest way of gathering data is by examining the waste a company generates, it is known as "dumpster diving".

Such measures will make it more difficult for competitors or even foreign intelligence agencies to gain access to company secrets. However the main weakness remains the employee who is willing to break and circumnavigate such rules. Besides ensuring that no clearly rotten apples are employed by screening candidates in advance and on a regular basis, the real key to fighting information loss and any criminal activity within a company is by laying down clear rules and communicating such rules.

Employees need to understand why such rules are enforced and what the consequences are if these rules are broken. There has to be a clear zero tolerance policy for those breaking the rules which are enforced from the top down as rigorously as it is from bottom up. Many companies have such programs, most of them are however not effective as they tend to be computer based multiple choice questionnaires which are seen as a necessary evil.

In some cases employees are required to sign off on the rules governing information protection and other compliance issues, more often enough such declarations are signed without understanding why the rules have been drawn up. More effective are regular face to face workshops where senior management explains in detail the reasons behind such rules and the consequences of not living these rules. If this is done professionally and often enough then such measures, combined with other security measures, will result in a high degree of protection from criminal behavior in the company and a higher degree of business protection.

The risks companies face have increased significantly in the past years due to globalization and the advent of the internet and networked systems. Risk levels are likely to increase and new risks will emerge in the future. At the same time national and international law is requiring companies to run their operations in a manner compliant with such laws. Increasingly, companies are being investigated for infringing and breaking such laws, with significant financial and reputational consequences.

The fight against corruption, industrial and economic espionage and other economic crime is as much a battle against those wishing to attack your company as it is a fight for the hearts and minds of the employees.

Trade secrets and trade secret laws are essential parts of the corporate realm. Nearly 80% of the values of the Standard & Poor's 500 companies consist of intangible assets. Of that 80%, nearly 70% were created from ideas individuals had gained from previous employment. The most important aspect to classifying information as a trade secret is that it becomes protected from theft during the research and design phase of development.

Trade secret cases are often the least likely to result in a criminal trial because companies fear that during the discovery process of a trial, the competitor will be able to gather even more information about the intellectual property due to the prosecuting company having to disclose any and all relevant information. Although the above stated techniques are often used to protect a company's assets, they are not 100% effective.

These techniques can be used in combination or in part in order to reduce the likeliness of becoming a victim of economic espionage. While patents, copyrights, and trademarks help to protect against established goods and services, trade secrets are essential to help protect companies during the research and design phase of product development.

There are many types of information that is sought after by criminals engaging in economic espionage. When referring to information, it is important to understand that not only is organized data sought after, but any piece of information that could impact an organization if it becomes compromised by the wrong individual.

For example, even source code can be considered a trade secret as long as it is classified as a trade secret and derive independent economic value which was decided in USA v. Aleynikov. Information can come in many different forms and varieties. Information sought after by criminals can be technologically sophisticated to simple forms of paper, and even trash.

First, technology based information is the most common form in which information is stored. Specifically related to computer based information is e-mail. E-mail creates great risks for companies; most people using it do not think about how they are using it.

This technological advancement is used to transmit all types of corporate information and is easily accessible by white collar criminals. Simple computer hacking (i.e. accessing the e-mail server), or just observing an open e-mail (or a paper print out of the message) on an unattended computer can have devastating effects to organizations.

Second are formal documents that are used by companies for a variety of purposes. These must all be printed out and kept as hard-copy documents, stored most commonly in file cabinets. Third are draft documents, which are often referred to as "worthless".

Most people assume that once the final product is produced, draft documents hold no value. The information these documents contain can be highly valuable. Fourth are working papers, the precursors to formal documents. Again, these documents are often thought of as not valuable, but they often contain information and specifications of outlining projects. Fifth are scrap papers, which are almost always thought of as invaluable. Scrap paper often contains parts of the final project on different pieces of scrap. If a criminal can collect scrap, he/she may be able to put together the pieces of the whole to gain information and harm the company.

Internal correspondence, legal and regulatory filings, other records, and the media are all types of information that corporations use to spread information. Internal correspondence contains a substantial amount of information pertaining to a company's intellectual property. Internal correspondence is used to share information within an organization through the use of newsletters, policy documents, or meeting minutes.

This spread often contains highly sought after information in order to keep employees informed on company growth, such as legal and regulatory filings. Legal and regulatory filings are documents that companies are legally required to produce. These filings and documents are often revealing to companies trade secrets and become accessible by anyone under the Freedom of Information Act (FOIA).

Other records, such as hotel, airline, and car rentals, are highly sought after by economic espionage spies. These records help the spies track targets and plant tracking or eavesdropping devices to follow and record possible confidential business transactions. Almost anything anyone does in today's technologically advanced world creates a record that can create vulnerabilities for companies.

Also important in the theft of trade secrets is media or open source information. This is anything that is publically available for viewing or direct access. In other words, this is a form of competitive intelligence, the process of legally gathering information to understand the competition within the global market.

Without the use of competitive intelligence, companies would easily become obsolete. Another type of information is corporate communication. There are three main types of corporate communication: formal meetings, informal meetings, and casual conversations. Formal meetings often contain the most sensitive information regarding intellectual property.

These meetings often include the highest officials within an organization and discussions of future plans and developments. Informal meetings are anytime employees get together to talk about work either in person, over the telephone, or a gathering in a common area.

The information discussed in these informal meetings ranges greatly and can include sensitive corporate information. Lastly, and the most overlooked, is casual conversations. These types of conversations usually take place in open, public places where there is no expectation of privacy, as is the case with the other two types of communication

. These classifications of information are important in understanding how criminals access sensitive information. As identified by the literature, the most common ways in which sensitive material is accessed are from the types of information that are deemed the least important by both the corporation and its employees.

These types of information can be email, casual conversations, and/or scrap paper. These are often the easiest for criminals to access because they are the most common forms of business transactions. Even though the three types of information are often overlooked as valuable, it is important for a company to work to protect all types of information. In order to reduce the likelihood that a company, organization, or individual may become victimized, there needs to be the use of risk evaluation.

3. THE ROLE OF TECHNOLOGY IN EXTENTION OF ECONOMIC ESPIONAGE

During the 20th century, the intelligence community resulted in the development of information technology. Modern telephone networks and computers have both originated in this way. Today, the intelligence community is no longer at the cutting edge of development and research in the information world. The largest problem is the failure to keep up with changes in how modern societies use information and how information technology shapes the world.

Economic information has been a target of espionage especially for nations with less developed industrial capabilities. The different kinds of information that are important to nations are constantly expanding to economies and other areas where it is difficult to guard information. Economy is the backbone of functioning societies as well as international relations.

Political entities need networked, active and dependable economic systems. Economic espionage has the same importance for a country's economic interests as more familiar types of espionage have for traditional political and security interests.

The traditional concept of espionage may be seen as a contest between opposing states, which is rooted in the concept of the nation state that is built on the idea of one sovereign power controlling a certain territory. This model assumes that any information about the nation state in question is the property of that state. The citizens of a nation who spy against the interests of their own state endanger its sovereignty and exhibit disloyalty against their government.

Where the nation state is responsible for giving its citizens protection against violence and a stable and structured society, the people being governed by the state are implicitly expected to be loyal to their governments.

Today identities are formed increasingly by religion, ethnicity and other personal attributes that have rendered the nation state model obsolete to some extent. In addition, this trend has pushed corporations into fields of influence formerly occupied by states alone. In a world of increasing globalization these notions about espionage among the system of nation states can be said to no longer hold the same weight as before.

It has therefore been suggested that power is less vested in territorial hegemony backed up by military strength and more in how successfully the citizens of a given state participate in the global economy. This brings into question the loyalty of the individuals who take part in the global economy through multinational companies, banks and independent agencies. Today's intelligence activity is formed by the powerfully growing multitude of information in the world and at the same time by the increased access to information via the internet and other computer networks.

The possibilities of acquiring both open source and secret information through signals surveillance, internet monitoring and data trespasses have maximized. Parallel to these methods, also traditional covert practices such as coded messages, agent recruitment and pressure against individuals are used to a larger extent. Technological development has activated new non-state intelligence actors.

It can be hard to assess to what extent espionage is supported by any given state, and there have been cases where suspicions have arisen that information collection has not always been initiated by the country that carries out the activity, but that it is in fact acting on behalf of a third party. Regardless of the actors involved the consequences for those hurt by information loss can be great.

The global economy has changed the way actors identify friends and enemies who would spy on them. The bipolar system of the Cold War kept espionage among allied nations in check. In today's world there is an abundance of possible customers for information.

One scenario of the future anticipates that those who succeed in the global economic competition will share information and work together to grow both their individual and economic powers. While these kinds of groups are still in the process of forming, it is already clear that they will gravitate towards the most advantageous positions available thus potentially ignoring historical alliances or values.

By stealing plans for the Harrier jet, the BI-B bomber, the American Airborne Warning and Control aircraft and the MK-48 torpedo as well as several air and ground radars, the Soviets saved millions of dollars in research and development. As Soviet military technology advanced, The

North Atlantic Treaty Organization (NATO) was forced to undertake new research projects in order to keep its qualitative advantage over the East. This escalated the arms race and thus contributed to the overall elevation of the Cold War. While claims such as these are difficult to evaluate, they indicate a perception that some intelligence services and their respective governments seek actively to benefit from industrial espionage.

Recently China has been the country most often associated with industrial espionage. The main reason for this is the rapid industrial development in Asia. As the Asian market grows, more companies are placing their production there and at the same time Asian companies and researchers are working abroad. The fixed costs connected with research and development can be reduced through successful economic espionage. For example, if the production technology of a foreign company is acquired through clandestine means, domestic firms will benefit from lower costs and also achieve a strategic benefit in the global markets.

After the Cold War the need for military intelligence staff diminished and industrial intelligence started to employ a larger part of the professional intelligence officers. When the economic depression of the early 1990s was over, trade and industry regained their strength as industrial espionage grew into an even more central and critical factor. The constantly increasing value of trade secrets and the quick expansion of technology have created a large increase in the motives, possibilities and activities of industrial espionage.

These efforts are not only aimed at finished products and marketable ideas, but also towards the processes themselves that generate them. Samuel Porteous has drawn attention to the lack of a coherent terminology in dealing with issues related to economic and industrial intelligence. He has defined economic intelligence as "the policy or commercially relevant economic information, including technological data, financial, proprietary commercial and government information, the acquisition of which by foreign interests could, either directly or indirectly, assist the relative productivity or competitive position of the economy of the collecting organization's country".

Most economic intelligence gathered by governments and companies is collected legally from open sources using overt methods. The use and collection of information in this manner, which may be done through visiting students, scientists or businesses, is a favorable feature of an open society and crucial to technological and economic development. Economic intelligence can however slide to the realm of economic espionage, when obtrusive and covert methods are used.

According to Porteous, economic espionage is "the use of, or facilitation of, illegal, clandestine, coercive or deceptive means by a foreign government or its surrogates to acquire economic intelligence. The acquisition of an actual piece of technology, such as physical examples of technological information or documents, is assumed to be included in this definition". He further defines industrial espionage as "the use of, or facilitation of, illegal, clandestine, coercive or deceptive means by a private sector entity or its surrogates to acquire economic intelligence". When competitive intelligence is taken too far, it becomes economic espionage. Where business intelligence deals with legally available information in an analytical manner, industrial espionage is essentially about stealing corporate secrets.

The terms of industrial espionage and industrial intelligence can be used interchangeably, and are understood to encompass the same essential characteristics of illegal intelligence activity.

Many intelligence services support their nations' trade and industry, which can raise the vulnerability for different types of intelligence gathering. Technical development and advanced equipment lead to new ways of acquiring sensitive information. Despite a growing information leakage through technical equipment and surveillance, intelligence still very much happens through human sources.

Espionage and gathering are made possible through foreign persons who are officially stationed in the country, are employees with a company or through an official who sells information to a foreign power. A great deal of industrial intelligence gathering has been undertaken by former employees. It is not unusual that espionage is carried out by storing or sharing secret information on portable computers, memory sticks and mobile phones. This places great demands on modern information security, which has become one of the main elements in successful corporate security.

The responsibility of the individual has become more important during current times when the security of companies, officials and organizations depends on the security thinking of the employed. It has been estimated that approximately half of all information technology related crimes that happen could have been prevented if the existing security systems had been used properly.

The largest challenge is to adapt the previous security consciousness to the technical, mobile and international context of today. A number of intelligence services spend resources on improving their technical information gathering capacity, resulting in more discrete and efficient intelligence activities.

The transmission of more and more information via mobile means of communication, together with the increased integration of data and telephone communications, makes communication systems more vulnerable and increases the risk of computer intrusion, tapping and signals intelligence activities. Improved protection measures for sensitive or particularly vulnerable communication systems are necessary to counter such risks.

The growth of industrial espionage has been helped by the advances in the technical equipment applicable to covert information gathering. As for the perpetrators of industrial intelligence, we can divide the human sources into two categories. A covertly corrupted agent supplies information for compensation and sees nothing wrong in his actions.

An example of this might be someone who gets close to secret information in their job and discusses it with an outsider, while considering his actions to be for example a form of consultancy. A volunteer agent is someone who sells information for a price and knows he is engaged in illegal activity. His actions are usually planned and systematic. The volunteer agent is more likely to get caught than the covertly corrupted agent. There is also the danger that a potential customer can betray the agent to the authorities.

Most of the crimes involving trade secrets in Silicon Valley have been committed by employees and other persons working for the company. In short, it has been shown that the staff of a company is behind most information crimes and cases of industrial espionage.

The highest risk groups for corporate trade secrets include former employees, temporary staff, current employees, vendors or suppliers and consultants. In the Ericsson espionage case, the offenders were all volunteer agents inside the company.

Most people with access to classified information do not commit acts of spying. However, it has been suggested that certain people can be influenced by circumstances in their personal or professional lives to undertake illegal actions.

Moreover, people can be pushed to spy on their employers by emotional ties to foreign entities, personal discontent towards the employer or financial troubles. When for example a person experiences that he or she is not treated well by the employer it can be easier to rationalize the choice of engaging in espionage.

This self-rationalization was strongly present in the Ericsson case. A common method among intelligence services is to frequent fairs and conferences. To be able to talk with one or several researchers or representatives for firms in that situation under a visibly legitimate context, can give a lot of valuable information. Even stolen briefcases, computers and other equipment are utilized.

Another method of espionage among companies is the "lending" of an employee by one firm to another. The person in question then proceeds to learn the competitor's business secrets and later returns to his original employer. Espionage can also be carried out by disloyal employers, who feel that they have been mistreated or feel unhappy in some way.

With the rise of industrial espionage the security measures of companies have toughened. Together this with the intensified monitoring of employees brings distrust in the workplace.

The so-called mosaic method, where information fragments from different open and secret sources are pieced together can very well lead to the exposure of an entity that gives away information that would have otherwise remained secret.

Some intelligence services have systematized this approach through a network of visiting students and researchers from their country. Intelligence officers often seek to get close to personnel in defense, company directors, product developers, researchers and other bearers of attractive information.

Other nations' research institutes, companies, delegation visits and dissident circles are examples of traditional areas where an intelligence actor under cover or false identity can work through illegal or legal channels.

Industrial espionage is a security intelligence subject targeted by counterespionage. The largest element of risk in industrial intelligence has always been the human factor. Recent cases clearly show that companies risk the most damaging information losses via their staff.

Moreover, the fact that the storage and systematization of information nowadays takes place using technical aids has also facilitated individuals' access to large amounts of information. This means that intelligence organizations aspire to recruit human sources.

The recruitment of an agent is no coincidence, for it is preceded by careful studies where factors such as motivation, access and reliability are thoroughly assessed. Recruitment is always approved by the head office of the intelligence service.

The rapid advances in information technology have made it more difficult to restrict access to secret information. While information technology has increased the productivity of employees it has also given them new tools for espionage.

The storing of information in large databases that can be easily searched has made it easier to locate specific information. Another significant feature is the possibility of storing huge amounts of data on small portable devices.

The globalization of trade and research has facilitated the opportunities for industrial espionage by increasing cooperation between people from all over the world. This provides opportunities for recruitment as well as sharing and selling classified information.

Furthermore, counterintelligence is now faced with the difficult challenge of separating normal working relationships from those that could potentially turn into a security risk.

For example, scientific research is built on collaboration that in today's world is increasingly international in its nature. It can be very difficult to decide which information of a given project should be protected. If the economic power of a nation is understood to be as integral to national security as military power, how should the covert collection and use of industrial intelligence be handled?

Further questions rise if the government of a given nation decides to give economic intelligence to its national companies. How do multinational corporations fit into this configuration? Ultimately, we are facing a question of conflicting national loyalties.

In the United States, former Director of Central Intelligence (DCI) Stansfield Turner has suggested that making information public could diminish the edge a foreign company might have over a domestic one. This leads to the idea that the worlds of intelligence and business must strengthen their ties with the rise of economic importance.

Turner has arrived at the conclusion that global economic competition requires nations to spy on each other's economic secrets. This should be done in his view by technical collection rather than traditional human intelligence means.

The term innovation has been used mainly in the past to signify original scientific discoveries but in the current technology policy discourse it has expanded to include inventions that have possible marketable applications. An innovation system is organized action that strives to create, develop and exploit innovations.

In the context of the nation state the innovation system is called a national innovation system. Technology and knowledge have become key factors in the economy and are considered as important as economic growth, capital and work.

Within the framework of the national innovation system and technology policy, the private and public sectors and universities are expected to work together transcending institutional boundaries. Knowledge is now considered intellectual property as well as a potential product that can be exploited in the market.

This reconceptualization can be seen as the industrialization of the production of scientific knowledge. The universities are no longer the sole places producing new knowledge. The private sector will be more instrumental in creating technological advances than public sector actors while research and development will shift from the academic domain to companies. Research results are achieved in the process of knowledge production itself and in the movement of actors from one context of knowledge use to another.

This interdisciplinary research creates its own type of theoretical knowledge, practices and methods of inquiry. The quality of research is also increasingly measured in competition on the market and in terms of cost-effectiveness.

Innovative companies are the main drivers of economic growth in a knowledge-based economy in Finland and Sweden. Technology is the most important industry in Finland. It constitutes 60 % of Finnish exports and 75 % of research and development investments are directed towards the technology industry.

With the rapidly changing processes of technology diffusion and innovation, the national innovation and production systems are becoming more interdependent. The state is often the lead actor in promoting innovation through funding research and development as well as investing in technological applications. For example, innovation has been integral in the restructuring of the Finnish economy.

During the past 20 years, research and development intensity of Finland has grown to the second-highest levels within the European Union (EU) and the Finnish share of high-technology products to total exports among the highest in the industrialized world.

The geo-economic competition between nation states has become more important with deepening trade relations. Today, the struggle for trade secrets is a part of the national security of nations. However, this development has a contradictory effect where each nation strives to hold on to its comparative advantage or protect specific industries.

The role of intellectual property becomes not only important as a resource but also as a part of the national competitive advantage. This is especially vital for nations which invest in high technology development.

One example of the Finnish national innovation system has been the implementation of an alliance between companies, universities and the government called the triple helix model, which has helped to establish technology centers in cooperation with universities. The idea behind these centers is that the development of new technologies and the differentiation of customer-specific markets are understood to be the main reasons that drive companies to specialize further and create new kinds of knowledge and technologies.

For example in the 1990s, biotechnology centers were founded in six different locations around the country. The centers were established mainly through public funding by the Ministry of Education, The Finnish National Fund for Research and Development (Sitra) and the National Technology Agency (Tekes) that operates under the Ministry of Trade and Industry.

4. SOURCES OF RISK AND THREAT

In order for economic espionage to occur, there must be risk. "Risk is the driving consideration of all economic espionage activities". Risk is defined by the probability that company (or a person, in some cases) will become a victim of an undesirable event. In this context, there are several types of risk that an organization needs to consider. These risks can be organizational and/or reputational.

Organizational risk is what the organization stands to lose from the theft. Reputational risk is how the company's stakeholders and investors will be affected by the theft. For example, the trust that the company has with its investors will be tested if an occurrence of economic espionage is identified.

A threat is defined as a person, organization, event, or condition that could hurt a company in an undesirable manner, either man made or natural. A man made threat can be an employee. A natural threat can be things such as a floor or tornado, which may destroy buildings allowing direct access to sensitive information. Whenever a company or individual holds information that could possibly have value to someone or something else, the threat of economic espionage still exists.

Most threats are direct in nature, but they can also be indirect. For example, a company could possess information about another targeted company, which in turn makes the first company a secondary target. If two companies are working together to develop a new product, and one is a target, the other also becomes a target through association.

The largest and most common threats to any organization can be classified under the two broad categories of either human/man-made or natural. Organizations are vulnerable to theft by human adversaries. These human adversaries can be subdivided into internal and external adversaries.

Most importantly is that the loss of information can be unrecoverable and completely destroy a company. Threats can be internal employees, competitors, foreign competitors, and domestic competitors. As such, perils can damage reputation and lead to a loss of economic dominance, loss of stakeholders, and ultimately a loss of substantial income.

There are also different types of perils – the individual who leads to the threat. That is, the human adversary is responsible for the theft of valuable information. Human adversaries, meanwhile, can be classified into the broad categories of internal and external. Internal adversaries are specific to the employees of that organization or company.

These can be both current and former employees, and they are often very difficult to identify because companies often fail to recognize that a "trusted employee" may actually engage in a variety of nefarious actions that could expose the company to a variety of risks.

In fact, a typical internal spy may appear to be one of the hardest workers. A worker who does his/her job to a high level often never gets questioned or observed in-depth, making it easy for him/her to slip away with valuable information.

There are many reasons why internal employees may commit economic espionage, such as because they are: disgruntled, thrill seeking, or departing. Another major factor is the financial aspect. Individuals may engage in economic espionage to display how profitable a simple criminal act can be.

Former employees may engage in economic espionage out of vindictiveness, to receive a payoff, or to impress a new boss. Lastly, on-site non-employees, ideologues, and activists also pose a threat to companies. In other cases, internal threats may be compromised in some manner.

For instance, a common "Cold War" tactic was to place an employee in a compromising situation and then blackmail that individual for specific information. If nor extortion, in other cases, trusted employees are actually "tricked" by individuals where they inadvertently or purposefully provide an individual company secrets out of devotion or love.

In other cases, competitors themselves engage in economic espionage. Externally, competitors pose the biggest threat to companies' worldwide. A competitor is any business that seeks to gain control of the global market at the demise of another entity. Midsize companies face the largest competition and are less aware of possible threats because most hold the mentality that they are not large enough to be victimized or the information they possess has no intrinsic value.

More specific to the United States are its foreign competitors. The threat from foreign competitors is often complex. For example, "multinational corporations know exactly what they can and cannot get away with, and they become experts at covering their tracks".

Another example, multinational corporations know the nature and extent of the law and understand what is legal or illegal. If the action they desire to pursue is illegal, these corporations use techniques that are hard to detect and have the resources (financial stability) for an expert legal team to help protect them from legal prosecution.

More than 100 nations worldwide target the United States to carry out their acts of economic espionage. Many of the operations carried out against the United States are government funded, and the individuals are never held legally responsible, giving foreign nations a sense of immunity.

Most existing laws, for example, only protect domestic intellectual property, therefore, when economic espionage is committed internationally, it is not considered a crime. Secondly, when a different state is victimized, they hardly every take punitive action.

For example, when the United States were alerted of French spies being within the corporation of IBM, the United States responded by simply sending a letter of diplomatic protest. It is occurrences like these that do not create general deterrence and promote the continuation of economic espionage. Both hostile and allied nations are among many which target the United States for intellectual property.

Hostile nations are less concerned with political embarrassment when engaging in economic espionage against the United States. Without the fear of getting caught, these nations are far more likely to commit economic espionage than their allied counterparts.

These nations are willing to take more risks and use more aggressive, overt tactics. These hostile nations realize now that economic prosperity is more important than military intelligence, and are therefore making economic espionage an important part of their strategic plan.

The hostile nations are identified as: Russia, China, Iran, and Cuba. It is outstanding what these countries can do to companies in the US. For instance, a more obvious and well known tactic used by the former USSR was the installment of the KBG in foreign Nations worldwide to gain access to intellectual property.

In a more covert manner, China employs intrusive measures through the use of visiting students and professors. They use these students and professors to infiltrate corporate and academic laboratories and send their findings back to the Chinese government.

The United States' allies are some of its greatest competitors not only in the global market, but also within the American economy. Nearly all of the nations considered to be United States' allies target the United States for intellectual property. Of the many allied nations that target the United States, there are a few that do it on a regular, more extreme basis. These nations are: Japan, France, Israel, and Germany.

Many counties which have been military allies of the United States are in fact at "war" with the United States economically. These countries include England, France, Germany and Israel. For example, France "bugged" first-class cabins of Air-France planes to record the conversations of international businessmen, allowing them to monitor the conversations of high class corporate executives.

In these cases, the country itself might engage in espionage using the resources of the nation, or the state may employ agents to target certain companies and even universities to steal intellectual information that can be later used in the military and economic development of that particular country.

Organized crime groups can be found throughout both the United States and worldwide. Some of the most popular organized crime groups can be identified as the Italian Mafia, the Eastern Bloc mafias, and drug cartels. Organized crime groups most often pose a minimal threat but still have damaging capabilities. Most often, organized crime groups are often found involved in economic espionage when their services are contracted by an organization to steal from its competitors.

The most common techniques that these organized crime groups use are computer hacking and misrouted transactions. For example, Russian crime rings have stolen $1 billion from the United States over hacked computer networks.

There are other smaller, less organized forms of threats that organizations and individuals should be made aware.

First and foremost is petty crime. The criminal, for example, may steal a personal computer and unknowingly have also stolen intellectual property that could be valued much higher than the personal computer itself.

More specifically, in 1997, a thief targeted Levi Strauss & Co. and managed to steal a computer hard-drive from the company. On this hard-drive were the names, birthdates, and social security numbers of thousands of employees. A more recent example, during the period 2006 to 2012, the Western District of Pennsylvania indicted a group of five Chinese nationals who had either conspired to or actually hacked into United States' companies in order to benefit Chinese competitors. This group of individuals each planned to hack into American entities and maintain access to their computer networks in order to steal information.

Secondly, hackers also pose a threat to any organization. Hackers are individuals who have an in-depth understanding of the internet and how the internet functions. The fear that hackers present to organizations gives hackers the persona that they are unstoppable.

However, most hackers are simply curious and want to explore and discover things on the internet; they like to test their individual skills to see if they are capable of breaking into protected systems. Hackers will often exploit vulnerabilities that cannot be fixed. A hacker will be able to break through a computer firewall because the software unknowingly has a weak point that cannot be fixed.

For example, a skilled hacker can write code and run applications; these are most common to be continuous and automated. One of the biggest motivations for hackers is, in fact, economic espionage. Hackers often gain access to an organization's system without company knowledge and do so for an extended period of time. Once the desired information is obtained, hackers are able to remove all traceable evidence, making it difficult for hackers to be caught and criminally prosecuted.

Hackers are constantly evolving and perfecting their abilities, which contributes to their effectiveness and makes them hard to detect. In today's advanced technological society, there are numerous threats that will continue to occur without recognition. All nations, both hostile and allied, target the United States for the vast intellectual property its organizations hold. Often times, organized crime groups do not pose a large threat unless they are contracted by another organization to steal from competitors. Lastly, hackers and petty crime pose a minimal threat, unless by chance, the individual unknowingly comes across intellectual property.

Once threats have been identified, an organization must understand its vulnerabilities in order to better safeguard its intellectual property. Vulnerabilities are the weaknesses in an organization's security functions. The fewer 28 vulnerabilities a company contains, the less likely it is to have risk. The best way to succeed at reducing risk is to understand organizational weaknesses, and how criminals access valuable information. Organizations face operational, physical, personnel, and technical vulnerabilities.

Operational vulnerabilities are weaknesses that result from an organization's daily tasks. These are most likely to precede an occurrence of economic espionage. Operational vulnerabilities are: poor awareness of preexisting security operations, social engineering, accidents and carelessness, poorly developed policies and procedures, predictability, failure to act on sound procedures, detailed sales and marketing, public relations, and lastly, giving out too little information.

Social engineering for example, is when a person acts as if he/she is in a trusted position in order to receive passwords from employees. Predictability refers to a company's routine, and doing the same action in a repetitive manner. Detailed sales and marketing affects a company when they release too much information about an upcoming and newly developed product. Lastly, giving out too little information can create vulnerabilities for a company by giving the appearance that the company may be hiding something valuable.

These operational vulnerabilities, coupled with physical vulnerabilities, make it difficult for a company to safeguard its assets. When physical security comes to mind, most individuals think of uniformed patrol officers, fenced property, electronic locking doors, and heavy iron doors that seem to be impenetrable. However, physical security is defined as, physical measures "designed to safeguard personnel; to prevent unauthorized access to equipment, installations, material, and documents; and to safeguard them from: espionage, sabotage, damage and theft".

With the criminal act of economic espionage, the physical security component to protecting one's assets is much more in depth and includes many components that are often overlooked. Physical vulnerabilities related to economic espionage include, but are not limited to: poorly informed guards, lacking access controls, garbage (i.e., not shredding valuable materials), open storage (i.e., not locking file cabinets), information storage (i.e. password protected computers and logins), copy machines (i.e., leaving copied information on the printer), neighbors (i.e., eavesdropping), loss of control due to natural disaster, smaller equipment style (i.e., smaller equipment is easier to conceal and steal), no regularly scheduled audits, messy desks (i.e., hard to notice when important things go missing), leaving valuable information in mail boxes, not logging off computers, lack of the use of available locking equipment, power failure, and placement of building and equipment (i.e., a computer by an open window is easier to steal). In collaboration with physical and operational vulnerabilities, an organization must also consider personnel vulnerabilities and technical vulnerabilities.

Personnel vulnerabilities are similar to operational vulnerabilities. Personnel vulnerabilities are "related to the ways in which companies hire and manage their employees". These can include, but are not limited to: failure to validate claimed backgrounds, susceptibility to criminal behavior, and isolation of human resources and personal hardships. Technical vulnerabilities are related to an organization being victimized without having to be on the premise.

Technical vulnerabilities can include: configuration errors, which leave unintentional access points for criminals; poor password creations; difficult to detect system modifications (i.e. the more complex the system, the harder it becomes to detect changes); easily accessible modem; poor data storage; data transmission across computer 30 networks' virtual computer access (i.e. accessing computers from hundreds of miles away); electromagnetic pulse; wire taps; and bugs (i.e. small electronic recording devices).

With so many vulnerabilities of which companies have to be aware, it is virtually impossible for a company to be impenetrable. Not only do companies have to be concerned with internal vulnerabilities, but they must be aware of vulnerabilities that may go undetected.

Undetected vulnerabilities are the most damaging to companies worldwide. Company risk, combined with a high amount of vulnerabilities, leads to the occurrence of economic espionage; therefore, a company or entity must institute counter measures.

Although this is not always the case due to a company's reputational risk, once a company feels that it has been a victim of economic espionage or theft of trade secrets, the company may report it to any law enforcement agency.

Once the complaint is made, the US Department of Justice, in particular, the Federal Bureau of Investigation, may become involved. This federal agency, along with Department of Justice, is responsible for arresting and prosecuting the individual, or individuals, responsible for this criminal act. Although this process seems relatively simple, companies may be hesitant to bring about a criminal conviction due to the discovery process and their reputation. There are many reasons for not reporting.

The most common reasons are negative publicity, embarrassment, the threat of losing future investors, shareholder frustration, and further exposure of other trade secrets during the prosecution process. For these reasons, the true extent of the worldwide problem of economic espionage and trade secret theft is hard to determine. These crimes are often difficult to assess due to the "dark figure of crime," which is unreported crimes to criminal justice officials.

Although the problem is often underreported, there are several factors that have led to this steady increase in occurrence. One of the major contributing factors is due to the insurmountable pressure for economic dominance. Many organizations, and even nation states, resort to economic espionage in order to maintain a competitive level within the world market. Because of this pressure to gain economic dominance, companies have moved away from leadership, concerns with resources, and productions costs.

Companies who are in need of gaining economic dominance may engage in criminal activities rather than ethical means. Now, the goal of corporations is to dominate the world market at all costs and have a strong emphasis on management and market composition. Secondly, companies who lack the resources necessary to generate corporate intellectual capital engage in economic espionage or trade secret theft in order to compete in the competitive world market.

In fact, it is just as important to generate corporate intellectual capital as it is to be the first company to market a new product. Smaller, less sophisticated companies do not have the time and resources available to generate intellectual capital; therefore, they are more likely to engage in economic espionage or trade secret theft.

Lastly, the lack of protection and globalization make intellectual property easily accessible to competing companies. Because of the increase in occurrence of economic espionage, legislators created laws to try to combat and deter the commission of economic espionage.

In USA, prosecutions involving the theft of trade secrets were tried under tort violations in civil court. In particular, there were the protections of patents, copyrights, trademarks, and trade secrets. At the state level, there is the Uniform Trade Secrets Act, the National Stolen Property Act, the World Trade Organization, and the Trade-Related Aspects of Intellectual Property Rights Agreement. At the federal level, different attempts have been made to help companies protect their valuable assets.

The National Stolen Property Act of 1948 was among the forefront of federal statutes to combat trade secret theft.

The National Stolen Property Act, which was enacted by the United States in 1948, "prohibits the transportation, transmission, or transfer of any goods, wares, merchandise, securities, or money of the value greater than $5,000, knowing the same to have been stolen, converted, or taken by fraud".

Due to the narrow scope of the law, trade secret theft prosecutions were unsuccessful. This was because the law was initially directed at property crime, not intangible property such as trade secrets. Stemming from the World Trade Organization, the Trade-Related Aspects of Intellectual Property Rights Agreement provided members of the World Trade Organization dispute resolution.

Civil suits were also often used to gain compensation from losses, but these were not applicable to all victims. For example, small businesses might spend more in legal fees in comparison to the value of their financial losses. With all of these failed attempts to combat and deter individuals from engaging in economic espionage and theft of trade secrets, major legislative reform was necessary to enhance the effectiveness of prosecution.

In 1979, the Uniform Trade Secrets Act was enacted to create the first attempt at an all-inclusive legislation to combat trade secret theft.

The Uniform Trade Secrets Act (UTSA) allows a party to sue and recover stolen assets from a third party, both civilly or criminally. Criminal prosecutions can result from theft of misappropriation of trade secrets. The victimized company can attempt to criminally prosecute the offender, and if it feels as though it did not receive enough compensation, the victimized company can file a civil lawsuit.

A total of 42 states have attempted to enact state laws modeled after the Uniform Trade Secrets Act, but they have shown to be unsuccessful due to the lack of resources needed at the state level. In combination with the lack of resources, lack of uniformity creates confusion as to what economic espionage is and how it should be tried at the state level. Therefore, the Economic Espionage Act (EEA) of 1996 was created as a federal law to help companies protect their intellectual property.

5. THE ECONOMIC ESPIONAGE ACT (EEA) OF 1996

The Economic Espionage Act (EEA) of 1996 was signed into law by President Bill Clinton on October 11, 1996. EEA was created to criminalize the theft of trade secrets and increase the likelihood of preservation of investments. The major goal of the EEA was to maintain fair market competition and prevent corporate spies from stealing from their competitors. The Economic Espionage Act of 1996 gave way to a more specific definition of the term "trade secret".

The act created two new federal crimes with respect to theft of trade secrets. These laws are cited under section 1831 and 1832 of the EEA. The EEA consists of eight subsections, §1831-1839, prosecuting cases of economic espionage under section 1831 and 1832.

Section 1831 Section 1831 is directed against foreign countries. It provides more severe penalties if the offender had intent to benefit a foreign government, foreign company, or foreign agent by stealing trade secrets. In order for the government to have a successful conviction under section 1831, it has to prove three items. First, the government must prove the defendant, "knowingly possessed, received, or bought a trade secret".

Secondly, the government must prove that the defendant knew the trade secret was obtained illegally. Lastly, the government must prove the defendant intended or knew that the theft of trade secrets would benefit a foreign entity.

Section 1832 Section 1832, Theft of Trade Secrets, is the more general of the first two sections. Section 1832, "makes it illegal for a person to, among other things, possess a stolen trade secret with the intent to convert that trade secret to the economic benefit of anyone other than the owner thereof". There are three elements of intent required under section 1832. First, "the defendant must knowingly commit one of the listed acts of misappropriation".

Next, "the defendant must act with intent to convert a trade secret to economic benefit of anyone other than the owner thereof." Finally, "the defendant must act with the intentions of knowing the offense will injure any owner of that trade secret". The penalties associated with section 1832 vary depending on mitigating and aggravating circumstances. None the less, penalties for benefiting a foreign entity are much more severe than committing one for a personal gain.

In an effort to increase deterrence and reduce the amount of theft that companies of the United States face each year, congress imposed the Foreign and Economic Espionage Penalty Enhancement Act of 2012on January 14, 2013.This act increased the maximum fines for foreign and economic espionage to not more than $5 million for individuals and not more than $10 million or 3 times the value of the stolen trade secret.

This law also allows for review by the United States Sentencing Commission. The sentencing commission can review, and if applicable, change the sentencing guidelines and policy in order for the punishment to be more suitable for those persons convicted of offenses relating to economic espionage.

A significant gap has existed in trade secrets law for many years. Given the increasing importance of trade secrets in the Information Age, one would expect to see strong and effective criminal laws protecting the investment of industry in research and development.

Instead, only a minority of states have specifically criminalized the theft of trade secrets, under widely varying standards.

Moreover, the specialized resources necessary to investigate and prosecute this sort of crime have generally not been available at the local level. Federal law has not provided an effective remedy either, since the depression-era statute covering interstate transportation of stolen goods has been held inapplicable to "intangible" intellectual property.

Violations under both sections of the EEA are treated as serious crimes. Section 1832 provides for a term of up to ten years in prison and unspecified fines for individuals violating the EEA, and fines of up to $5 million for corporations or other organizations that violate its provisions.

The amount of the fine imposed on individuals is not specified, which means that the general maximum fine for felonies ($250,000) should apply. The legislative history suggests that, pursuant to the federal fines provision (18 U.S.C. § 3571(d)), the fine in cases of significant injury should be set at the greater of twice the value of the loss to the trade secret owner or twice the gain to the infringer.

The legislative history also suggests that organizations could be fined more than $5 million in cases where the loss to the trade secret owner was particularly high, by relying on section 3571(d) rather than section 1832(b).

Section 1831 provides for an enhanced penalty in cases of foreign espionage-- the maximum prison term is raised to fifteen years, and the maximum organizational fine is set at $10 million. The maximum fine for individuals is set at $500,000, rather than the normal felony maximum of *202 $250,000. Evidently, the general approach of the statute is to punish foreign espionage more severely than domestic trade secret theft.

Section 1834 additionally provides for forfeiture of a defendant's property during sentencing.148 Forfeiture of "any property constituting, or derived from, any proceeds the person obtained, directly or indirectly," from the theft is apparently mandatory.

By contrast, while the EEA also provides for forfeiture of "any of the person's or organization's property used ... to commit or facilitate the commission of the offense," forfeiture of such instruments is discretionary rather than mandatory.

The proceeds and instruments in question are forfeited to the United States, rather than to the victim of the crime. However, the Congressional Record suggests that victims may be able to seek restitution from the United States out of the forfeited proceeds.

Section 1834(b) of the EEA provides that, with certain minor exceptions, the forfeiture of proceeds and instruments shall be governed under the laws relating to drug forfeitures. Those laws vest title to the seized property in the United States, and provide that the Attorney General shall dispose of those assets "by sale or any other commercially feasible means."

Where the assets seized include the misappropriated trade secret itself--for example, where the secret is embodied in a product--the victim of the trade secret theft has a potential problem. Under section 1834, the government is granted title to the product embodying the victim's trade secret, and indeed has a mandate to auction that product to the highest bidder.

This is hardly consistent with the victim's interest in keeping the information secret. The victim's best recourse in such circumstances is to proceed under section 853(n) of the drug forfeiture statute, which specifies a procedure whereby the victim can petition the court to return all forfeited property in which the victim claims an interest.

Alternatively, the victim could seek to have the infringing goods destroyed, as is done with drugs. Either of these two options seems more probable than public sale. It is unlikely that the government, having acted to preserve a trade secret, would then risk destroying it by public sale of goods or documents embodying that secret.

A different sort of problem is presented by the seizure of a defendant's products, where the products do not directly incorporate a stolen trade secret, but are instead indirectly derived from misappropriated knowledge. This situation is likely to arise in cases involving "negative know-how."

The broad language of the forfeiture statute requires the government to seize "any property constituting or derived from, any proceeds the person obtained, directly or indirectly, as the result of such violation."

This strongly suggests that such derivative products are subject to seizure and sale, despite the intervening contribution of the defendant's own employees. Finally, section 1836 provides that the Attorney General may file a civil action to obtain "appropriate injunctive relief" in federal district court against any violation of the EEA.

Because this is a civil action, it might be stayed if there is also a pending criminal proceeding, as often happens in state civil trade secret actions. However, the government can use its injunctive power during the initial stages of prosecution to maintain the status quo or prevent public disclosure of a victim's secret.

On balance, the deterrent effect of a pending criminal action is such that preliminary injunctive relief will rarely be necessary: no reasonable lawyer would advise her client to continue to engage in conduct that is the subject of an indictment. In some circumstances, such as those where the defendant's conduct does not rise to the level of a criminal violation, civil injunctive relief may prove to be an appropriate substitute for criminal punishment.

In other cases, particularly those with foreign defendants, federal civil injunctive relief may be able to reach further than injunctive relief under existing state trade secrets laws. For the majority of cases, however, section 1836 adds little--besides federal court jurisdiction--to what can already be accomplished using state law.

6. THE PROTECTION FROM ECONOMIC ESPIONAGE

Protecting a company against economic espionage, or the theft of trade secrets, is not a simple task. In fact, it is possibly the most difficult task a company faces. Trade secrets are loosely protected by both state and federal laws and can be expensive for companies to protect their valuable assets. Simple and relatively inexpensive measures to help combat the occurrences are as follows.

There are four factors to be considered when implementing protection measures: size of company, risks within the business, history of security problems, and industry and/or government standards. The first step is to identify company information that would be valuable to competing companies and keep this information confidential.

Hannah (2005) identifies two types of protection procedures commonly used in corporations. The first is the use of access restriction, which restricts certain areas and prohibits employees from entering these areas. The second method is handling procedures, which state what employees can and cannot do when in contact with company trade secrets.

These employee restrictions should be present in protection measures to help contain the spread of information by employees. Employees who understand company policies and guidelines help safeguard against victimization by understanding what is allowed and the possible sanctions for misappropriating information.

Lastly, Pushkar (2005) identifies employment agreements. These consist of the employee reading guidelines and restrictions, which limit access and movement of intellectual property. Employees should then sign a document stating that they have read and understand policies and procedures and will not misappropriate valuable information.

Covenants, which are employee signed agreements not to disclose information received on the job, are also used as an attempt to keep employees loyal to their company during and after employment.

Winkler (1997) expands on these techniques and gives a detailed explanation of steps companies should take in order to reduce the risk associated with competing in a global market. Organizations should create awareness training programs, classify valuable information, install security alert systems, offer reward programs, require sensitive information to be transmitted on a face-to-face basis, verify access to rooms and computer networks, and verify identity of employees.

Employee badges should have no personal identifiers, and employees should sign agreements, releases, and be briefed on how to handle sales representatives and suspicious activity. Employees should not use cellular phones, and conversations outside of work should not include company information. Employees should alter daily work routines, include security in business meetings, involve security in policy updates, implement clear and sound disaster and incident procedures, and conduct penetration testing.

Corporations should conduct background checks on employees, check spouses and immediate family of employees, offer an anonymous employee hotline, maintain open lines of communication between departments, conduct audits, monitor visitors, classify employees, implement the use of locks and password protect electronic data, and remove clutter from the workplace. Corporations should also encourage the use of security reminders, shredders, locked trash containers, access control, anti-virus software, computer systems backups, multiple firewalls, bug and wiretap sweeps, and the use of encrypted data during transmission.

It should be noted that these safeguards are not fully effective, and the threat of being victimized still exists even with these precautions. By implementing these recommendations in part or in whole, the risk of victimization may be reduced. In fact, companies who take the proper steps to reduce vulnerabilities, will have less risk, in turn making that organization less desirable to criminals of white collar crime .

The research relating to economic espionage is relatively informative; however, it is limited. This research can generally be divided into three common areas: early industrial anecdotal stories, pre-EEA research, and post EEA studies. During the 1960s, concerns of economic espionage in advancing technological industries and the need for better protection of assets were among the forefront of research.

As time progressed, research began to focus on specific cases of economic espionage, theft of trade secrets, and the specifics pertaining to victimization and offender status.

In modern society, economic espionage is considered to be class two information warfare. Class two information warfare is related to how the stolen information is used, rather than how the information was acquired. Economic espionage is focused on how companies can gain a competitive advantage in large economic spheres rather than just gaining an advantage over one single competitor. Class one warfare, meanwhile, refers to attacks on an individual's electronic privacy.

China is one of the most common nations that engage in economic espionage. The Chinese have constructed corporate competitive intelligence programs to help China collect and steal intellectual property from the United States and other nations holding valuable information.

Slate (2009) found that the Chinese are experts at what they do. For instance, they have been known to be the world's leading product counterfeiters for over 300 years. As China seeks to compete with the United States in the world market, some of China's leading corporations will risk it all to acquire trade secrets and close the door on new technological advances.

The severe economic downfall in the 21st century felt around the world is affecting Chinese companies. As the situation continues to get 42 worse, and China's trade networks diminish, China feels the pressure to increase their participation in economic espionage in order to hold a strong hand in the world market and increase its gross domestic products (GDP).

Japan is also among the forerunners of committing economic espionage. Japan's economic espionage techniques are sponsored by the national trade organization, which sets goals and determines which trade secrets are worthy to steal. They most often carry out these attacks by sending students overseas to gain access to new developing technology. These students are often told for what to look.

Most of the techniques used by these students are taking photos and eavesdropping on conversations within university laboratories. In fact, in the 1990s, nearly two entire floors of a Manhattan skyscraper were reportedly occupied by Japanese intelligence spies in order to stay up-to-date on the latest technologies being developed in the

United States. It is also purported that the Japanese spies nearly destroyed the computer technology industry in Silicon Valley.

Aviation technology is another form of valuable information that attracts spies. The most likely country to engage in economic espionage with respect to airplane technology is France. France has had a long standing interest in the airline industry. For example, in order for the French national company of Airbus to gain a competitive advantage, industrial spies often targeted the United States' airline company, Boeing.

The French spies used communication receivers to intercept information that was transmitted from test flights conducted by Boeing. The most common endeavors in which French spies engaged were breaking into hotel rooms, stealing lap tops and brief cases, eavesdropping, and intercepting faxes and emails.

It is important to study economic espionage for a number of reasons. First, the occurrence of economic espionage causes companies great harm, not only financially, but it can also cost a company access to the competitive market. Economic espionage also impacts the

GDP of the United States and economic prosperity as a nation.

Companies not only invest time and money in the criminal process, but they also lose profits to the possibility of another company producing their product first. Secondly, it is important to study economic espionage because it can help companies safeguard their assets.

By understanding the frequency, victimization, and offender characteristics, the information produced can advise at-risk companies and help identify at risk employees.

7. THE ROLE OF CHINA IN ECONOMIC ESPIONAGE

In an environment of greater global economic interdependence, astounding technological advancement, the challenge of U.S. hegemony with the rise of new global superpowers, and the ease with which conflict and war can and have been waged, the nature of interstate relationships has never been more important. While U.S-China economic ties have significantly increased over the past three decades, the bilateral relationship continues to be riddled with complexities, friction, and tension.

The growing evidence of Chinese government complicity in commercial cyber espionage and theft of intellectual property (IP), costing the United States billions of dollars, has blurred the distinction between the geopolitical and economic realms, further complicating the relationship.

During bilateral discussions in June 2013, President Barack Obama warned Chinese President Xi Jinping that if cyber security issues, such as the theft of U.S. property, were not addressed, it would "be a very difficult problem in the economic relationship and was going to be an inhibitor to the relationship really reaching its full potential."

The possibility of this distrust spilling over into other areas of U.S.-China relations is a major concern that could determine whether the relationship becomes one of cooperation or more adversarial in nature. "Distrust of each other's actions in the cyber realm is growing between the U.S. and China," according to Kenneth Lieberthal and Peter Singer, political scientists and senior fellows at Brookings Institute.

The effect of cyber security on other aspects of the U.S.-China relationship is more important than with any other bilateral relationship because of the emerging world order and potential challenge to U.S. hegemony.

China is believed to have engaged in cyber espionage and intelligence collection as far back as 2004 when the Federal Bureau of Investigation (FBI) investigated intrusions, code-named Titan Rain, by Chinese hackers against U.S. military labs.4 In 2012, computer networks and systems around the world continued to be targets of intrusions and data theft, many of which originated in

China and were attributable directly to the Chinese government and military.

Though it would seem that China took a step in the direction of cooperation by agreeing in a 2013 United Nations report that international law does extend to cyberspace, there are no indications that China's cyber espionage and the theft of IP against the United States has waned.

China's cyber activity against the United States takes place in the context of an extensive economic interdependence between the two countries that could be seen as a source of accommodation and stability in the relationship. Taking into consideration the economic interdependence between the United States and China, the rise of China as a potential global power, and the threat of state-sponsored malicious cyber activity, the major question is: What does China's cyber behavior tell us about the role of economic interdependence in U.S.-China relations?

Other aspects of this question include: Is China's current use of cyberspace intended to shift the symmetry within U.S.- China economic interdependence and create a source of power for China? Does the use of cyberspace strengthen or weaken China's position within the U.S.-China relationship? How has China's cyber behavior been shaped by U.S.-China interdependence?

Economists agree that there is no emerging economy more important than China to the health of the global economy and that China will face difficult challenges that will require both economic and political change. Where economists diverge is in predicting whether China can maintain the significant growth seen of the last three decades to surpass the United States as the largest global economy and what that means for the global power structure.

"The next 40 years may see one of the greatest shifts in economic and military power in history," according to Uri Dadush, an author and economist with the Carnegie Endowment for International Peace. By 2050, the world's three largest economies will be the United States, China, and India. This shift in economic power will significantly affect global economic governance and regional and global interstate relationships.

However, "distortive economic policies that have resulted in over-reliance on fixed investment and exports for economic growth (rather than on consumer demand), government support for state-owned firms, a weak banking system, widening income gaps, growing pollution, and the relative lack of the rule of law in China" have been identified as potential weak points in China's economic development, according to a U.S. Congressional Research Service report. Predicting the economic growth or potential for any nation is difficult, but for China, it is especially difficult with the significant economic reforms identified in the country's Twelfth Five-Year Plan (FYP).

Similar to the degree of difficulty in predicting the economic growth of China, forecasting and analyzing China's behavior in cyberspace is equally problematic. There is no space more unpredictable than cyberspace, yet states are becoming increasingly dependent on information technology to drive political and economic development. The United States and China are two of the major players in cyberspace, but they hold vastly different views on acceptable behavior in the cyber domain.

Even among close allies, there is little consensus among researchers on what constitutes a cyber-attack or the threshold for an act of war in cyberspace. James Lewis, author and preeminent expert on cyber security, reasons that "an obstacle to managing cyber competition among states is the blurred boundaries between cyber-crime, cyber-espionage, and cyber-attack among states."

The Internet was originally designed for the free flow of information with security as an afterthought. "The only distinction between computer network exploitation and attack is the intent of the operator at the keyboard," argues Brian Krekel, author and subject matter expert on China.

Despite the difficulty in attribution of cyber operations and ability of a nation to potentially disguise cyber operations, the interdependence between two nations may be enough of a deterrence to prevent a cyber-attack. "Even when the source of an attack can be successfully disguised under a 'false flag,' other governments may find themselves sufficiently entangled in interdependent relationships that a major attack would be counterproductive.

China, for example, would itself lose from an attack that severely damaged the American economy, and vice versa," argues Joseph Nye, Distinguished Service Professor at Harvard University and co-founder of complex interdependence theory. But knowing where these lines are is a serious problem for both the United States and China. Offensive cyber operations require a deep knowledge of cultural or military sensitivities, potential "red lines," and how an attack or intrusion will be perceived.

For instance, China's government sees Tibetan exiles and Falun Gong hackers as national security threats, while the United States sees them as hacktivists advancing human rights and Internet freedom. Similarly, U.S. leaders view Twitter and YouTube as outlets for personal expression, but their Beijing counterparts identify the websites as instruments of attack.

In addition, cyberspace represents a domain in which a nation's economic, political, and military capabilities and vulnerabilities converge. The Internet thus may have no formal state borders, but it is increasingly a place that state entities both operate in and care deeply about.

IP, sensitive source code, proprietary data, business records, research and development, sensitive economic information, and advanced technology all exist in digital medium, enabling foreign actors to quickly gather massive quantities of data with little risk. The most important change facilitating economic espionage through cyberspace, or cyber-enabled economic espionage, is the sheer quantity of data produced digitally and stored electronically.

With China's long-term economic growth and prosperity riding on technological innovation, China's actions in cyberspace will be a major factor in determining future U.S.-China political and economic relations, as well as whether the rise of China as a regional hegemon will be peaceful.

While it would be difficult to say with any certainly what the future holds for U.S.-China relations or if China's ascent to great power status will be a peaceful one, China's cyber behavior does provides some indication about the role of economic interdependence in U.S.-China relations.

Over the last three decades, the United States and China have become heavily reliant on each other as a major source of economic growth. The United States has turned to China for its inexpensive goods and abundance of foreign capital to support its consumption model.

Similarly, China has turned to the United States as the world's single largest import market to support an export- and investment-led growth model. Two large economies had large gaps to fill and they quickly became hooked on what each could offer the other in their collective quest for economic growth.

Now intertwined in a somewhat balanced economic interdependent relationship, both the United States and China seek to manipulate the relationship in an effort to become the less dependent actor.

According to the WTO, the European Union is the largest import market in the world, but the United States is the single largest import market when looking at individual nations. Instead, through cyberspace operations, China has systematically conducted an economic espionage campaign against U.S. companies and government entities to acquire technology and IP and shift the economic balance of power in its favor.

China's theft of IP, costing the United States billions of dollars annually, clearly provides China an advantage.301 With China's push for increased indigenous innovation to strengthen economic development, cyber-enabled economic espionage allows China to bypass the costs of R&D and jump to the forefront of technological innovation by stealing other nations' hard work. As a result, China's cyber espionage threatens U.S. technological competitiveness and economic prosperity.

Although China denies accusations of cyber-enabled economic espionage, the capacity to conduct computer network exploitation operations to the extent that has been attributed to China is nearly impossible without some type of state-sponsorship.

Furthermore, China's Twelfth FYP and National Medium to Long-Term Plan for the Development of Science and Technology, 2006–2020 (MLP), both focusing on indigenous innovation and technological advancement, read like a cyber-espionage blueprint when compared directly to Chinese cyber intrusions and cyber-enabled economic espionage against the United States.

While the United States uses its power in the information domain to call attention to China's brazen cyber espionage behavior and gain collective support against China's cyber-enabled economic espionage, there are no indications the public exposure of Chinese cyber espionage has led China to stop its cyber-enabled economic espionage.

China has used asymmetric economic interdependence as a source of power and instrument of political coercion and China would likely be willing to do so against the United States should the economic balance of power shift in its favor. However, even if the United States becomes the more dependent party in the economic relationship, China's ability to use the asymmetry as a source of power will depend on United States sensitivity and vulnerability dependence to particular Chinese actions.

For instance, if after understanding the implication to its own economy China decided to use U.S. Treasury securities as a coercive tool against the United States by dumping mass quantities on the market in an effort to destabilize the U.S. economy, the United States would be sensitive to the immediate effects of U.S.

Yet, with the Federal Reserve prepared to purchase U.S. Treasuries dumped on the market in such a situation, the economic impact to the United States is significantly reduced as is its vulnerability to this particular Chinese action. Alternatively, if China decided to conduct cyber attacks against U.S. banks in response to U.S. trade sanctions or arms deals with Taiwan, devoid of any changes to U.S. policy, the United States would be substantially more vulnerable since U.S. government protection is in cyberspace is not extended to most of the private sector.

With the United States having articulated its intent to respond to serious cyber-attacks with a proportional and justified response in another domain, China's potential use of cyberspace to conduct offensive operations makes escalation of hostilities and the potential for conflict a real possibility.

American counterintelligence officials have noted that China has developed increasingly robust intelligence capabilities in recent years. Much has been written about China's diffuse intelligence activities, and observed trends in China's intelligence collection methodology have been well-documented, yet there remains much confusion amongst scholars and open source government publications regarding how and when China applies its techniques.

In recent years, Western nations have sought to label China's unique intelligence activities. Western governments, including the United States, often view China's HUMINT methods in contrast with the familiar tactics developed in Russia, Europe and the United States.

These methods, which have been loosely referred to as "traditional" intelligence methods by some in the United States government, might be characterized by the Cold War Russia v. US intelligence battles, in which trained agents of a government are employed to obtain information about a particular intelligence target.

Agents are trained by the government intelligence apparatus in tradecraft methods and are always cognizant of the role they play in collecting intelligence information on its behalf. Conversely, in the Chinese model, more people participate in intelligence collection, and each person obtains quantitatively less information than in so-called "traditional model".

Furthermore, it is unclear if all participants in Chinese intelligence are aware they are participating in intelligence collection. According to the Cox Commission Report, China frequently utilizes persons from outside the intelligence apparatus to provide information to the Chinese government.

This form of collection can take place by interviewing students with technical expertise, or inviting non-Chinese persons with the appropriate technical knowledge to travel to China and present information.

The diffuse and opportunistic use of non-service intelligence collectors often leads counterintelligence officials to describe China's intelligence capabilities as non-traditional or asymmetrical. For example David Szady, former head of the FBI's Counterintelligence Division, has stated that China's intelligence threat is: …increasingly asymmetrical insofar as it seeks to exploit the areas where there is a perception of weakness within the US national security approach and organizations.

Traditional notions of counterintelligence that focus on hostile foreign intelligence services targeting classified national defense information simply do not reflect the realities of today's complex international structure.

Another hypothesis posited by scholars and government officials is that China attempts to collect information through unclassified channels whenever possible, including collecting information that is perhaps not classified, but nevertheless has potential national security value, and seeks to take advantage of mistakes made through sloppy information security procedures.

Perhaps the most indicative of this theory is a book which was published by Chinese military experts regarding the Chinese military's intelligence collection methods and priorities. The manual, entitled, "Sources and Methods for Obtaining National Defense Science and Technology Intelligence," was published in 1991, and was the first comprehensive manual on China's overseas military espionage activities to be revealed to the West.

The manual focused predominantly on collection against US technology targets. The two authors of the book were Chinese military intelligence specialists. According to the book's translators, the book's dissemination was never restricted by the Chinese government, and contained surprising detail regarding the People's Liberation Army's intelligence collection methods.

Additionally, the book provided insight into China's perceptions regarding US culture and information weaknesses, for example displaying a general understanding of the open nature of US information, and advising its readers to take "fortuitous advantage" of opportunities to exploit loopholes in the American legal system and to uncover information leaks through media sources: Public materials are still a major source of intelligence for national defense S&T workers.

The Chinese government seeks to encourage the transfer of Western technologies to China, by legal and non-legal means. Recognizing the need to bolster China's technology position relative to more developed countries such as the United States, former Chinese paramount leader Deng Xiaoping instituted a plan called the 863 Program to foster the rapid development of technology needed to narrow the gap between China and the West in key science and technology sectors.

China's specific technology collection priorities were laid out in the 863 Program. According to the Cox report, the 863 Program was placed under the management of the Commission on Science and Technology in National Defense (COSTIND). The 863 Program budget is split between military and civilian projects, and focuses on both military and civilian aspects of science and technology.

In addition to the 863 Program, "the sixteen character policy" was created as China's blueprint for overt and covert efforts to buy, steal or otherwise acquire sensitive military technology. As described by the Cox Committee, the slogan urges China's science and technology planners to "combine the military and the civil; combine peace and war; give priority to military products; [and] let the civilian support the military."

The type of rapid technology acquisition described by the 863 Program cannot be achieved through completely organic means: to accomplish China's goals, outside assistance was sought, often through theft and replication of advanced technologies. The following section discusses the major intelligence services and other intelligence collectors which are responsible for executing China's technology collection efforts, and will highlight some of the ways in which China conducts traditional and non-traditional intelligence activities.

Unlike in the United States, where the intelligence collection mission is assigned to specific government agencies, in China information collection is a responsibility of many, if not all, government bureaucracies. However, there are several government agencies that are particularly important for China's foreign and domestic intelligence activities. This section describes some of the primary intelligence organs of the Chinese government and the extent to which they contribute to overseas technology collection.

China's intelligence method is unique because it implements a multipronged approach that allows its intelligence apparatus to make the most of its resources. China reserves its sophisticated, traditional espionage activities for situations that call for specialized access to information, and especially classified information. It relies on persons with little or no operational training individuals to conduct routine technology transfer operations, which seek restricted, but not classified, technologies.

China is able to conduct more operations in comparison to its Western counterparts in part because it does not use trained operatives for all, or even a majority, of its operations. The compromise with this approach is that more cooptees are at risk for exposure because they are not adequately disguised through rigorous operational security. And since China denies involvement in espionage activities abroad as a rule, those who risk their freedom to provide information to China are unlikely to get assistance from its government if they find themselves apprehended.

The Chinese approach poses many problems for U.S. law enforcement efforts, both because the frequency of China's non-traditional collection efforts tax the US law enforcement system's ability to keep pace with the activity, and because China's long-term, traditional clandestine technology collection efforts are, by design, difficult to detect.

An understanding of Chinese intelligence priorities will help counterintelligence officials to apportion its resources appropriately. In non-traditional cases, cooptees often only contribute small amounts of information, or only participate in a few operations.

8. LAWS OF CYBER WORLD

Cyber world is an extremely dynamic environment and it is not bound by physical laws. Cyberspace is constantly moving, and it has a high degree of complexity. Nowadays, cyberspace is accepted as a domain equal to land, air, sea, and space. In order to better understand the cyber environment and its peculiarities, certain principles must be presented.

According to Limnéll et all (2014), there are five fundamentals regarding to the laws of cyber environment. These are time, space, anonymity, asymmetry, and efficiency. Time is very relative conception in cyber world. In a sense, time loses its meaning in cyber word. Because of the Internet, malicious attackers can execute their attacks from anywhere around the world, without any time delay. Of course, the planning of the attack takes time, but the actual delivery of the attack is not bound by physical limits of time. The second fundamental is space.

Cyber world is neither bound by geographical distance, since almost everything is connected through Internet. Third concept is anonymity. Being anonymous in the Internet is a rather easy task. It is difficult to identify the attacker or hacker, and trace back the inception of the attack. If you are able to cover your tracks, there is no fear of being caught. The IP address of the attacker might be possible to track down, but it is impossible to say who is really using the address. In the anonymous cyber world, a same person can also use many different identities.

The fourth concept of cyber world is asymmetry. Cyber environment enables small actors to achieve large damage and serious harm against big players, such as global corporations or government entities. Hackers, criminals and terrorists can act all alone or in small groups, yet they can harass numerous different targets at the same time or put vast organizations on their knees. In cyber world, the attacker has a substantial advantage over the defender. Conducting a cyber-attack does not consume the attacker's resources, therefore attacks can be done persistently, and failures do not stop attackers from trying.

The last law of cyber world is efficiency, which is analogous to asymmetry of cyber world. In cyber environment, it is possible to perform many activities at the same time. A successful attack can infiltrate the network, compromise information, interfere connections, and sabotage critical infrastructure. The attack can manage to complete all these actions at the same time. The attacker's ability to accomplish many different activities at the same time, is a fundamental quality of cyber environment. These qualities make information risks unique and difficult to comprehend.

Information risks are crucial to understand, if an organization wants to survive in the new landscape of cyber threats. The objective of information risk management is to manage three basic attributes of information; confidentiality, integrity, and availability. Availability deals with the problems that information resources and data should always be available to the owner of the information, whereas integrity concerns the inviolability of information resources.

Regarding to trade secret thefts and economic espionage, confidentiality can be considered the most important attribute of information risk. Malicious insiders or external targeted threats are prone to offend the confidentiality of information assets.

Biener et all (2015), defines cyber risks as "operational risks to information and technology assets that have consequences affecting the confidentiality, availability or integrity of information or information systems".

Cyber risks derive from many different sources, from organization's operations and outside the organization. Basel III and Solvency II regulation frameworks categorize the sources of cyber risks in four different areas: (1) actions of people, (2) systems and technology failures, (3) failed internal processes, and (4) external events. The categories number 2 and 3 are technical by their nature.

Category number 4 includes external risks, such as natural and human catastrophes, regulatory compliance risks, market condition failures, and service dependencies. However, category number 1, actions of people, is where the trade secret threats derive from.

The actions of people category is divided to three different subcategories: 1. Inadvertent action, which is an unintentional action without malicious intent, such as error, omission and mistake. 2. Deliberate action towards organization's possession, such as fraud, theft, and sabotage. 3. Inaction, where employees fail to act due to their lack of skills or guidance.

Inadvertent actions constitute a large proportion of occurred information risks. Employees commit errors and omissions while they are working in haste. The number of error-based risks is larger than deliberate actions, but malicious theft and fraud are extremely injurious to organizations.

The legislation related problems are also encumbering the risk environment. The legislators of European Union have drawn up several information security related directives, which have been implemented to all member states. However, in European countries, such as in Finland, there is not a separate law that would govern information security.

Hence, there are acts, such as the Act on the Protection of Privacy in Electronic Communication (2004) and the Information Society Code (2014) that contain norms about information security. The largest obstacle in enacting a separate law is the fast development cycles of computer technology.

The state of perfect security is impossible to attain. Threats and vulnerabilities always exist, no matter how advanced the security systems are. This applies to both physical world and cyber environment. The challenge is to adjust the level of security to a sufficient level. The level is determined by every entity on its own initiative. A threat is anyone or anything that poses danger to the information security, where the target of the threat is information, computing resources, users, or data.

Threats can be divided into two categories; external and internal threats, depending on the source of the threat. Internal threats derive from inside the organization, such as the misconduct of employees. These threats arise from improper security policies, weak system and data administration, and the lack of security awareness.

External threats derive from outside the organization, especially from the environment in which the organization operates.

Cyber threats can be divided into two categories by the vulnerabilities they exploit; syntactic or semantic. Syntactic attacks exploit technical vulnerabilities, whereas semantic attacks exploit social vulnerabilities. However, many attacks have characteristics of both semantic and syntactic attack types. These blended attacks use technical tools to facilitate social engineering in trade secret threats.

Vulnerabilities are usually seen as unintentional failures that incur inside the network. However, vulnerabilities can be consequences of a deliberate act. Vulnerabilities are weaknesses that an attacker may exploit. In information security environment, these weaknesses are associated with security procedures, technical controls, physical controls or other controls of as- 16 sets.

Typically vulnerabilities are known as a technical issue, but humans as well cause significant part of the vulnerabilities, especially in the case of information confidentiality. Poor user account management is an example of important non-technical vulnerability, although it has technical attributes as well.

Sometimes human actions cause technical vulnerabilities. Software engineers are on a constant hurry to develop their programs to better serve their customers and launch programs before competitors. Therefore, the necessary amount of testing is many times left out from the developing process. This misstep sometimes leaves substantial defects to the programs.

One major source of vulnerabilities is software defects, also known as bugs. They usually cause abnormal functionality in software. An example of software bug is a buffer overrun, where a program accepts input without checking the size of it. The amount of data might be larger than the storage of the program has prepared for it. Therefore, the exceeding data will overwrite some other program storage, and the data can include malicious code.

A large amount of hacker attacks exploit buffer overruns. This vulnerability for example, is usually a deliberate act of a malicious attacker. There are of course unintentional technical vulnerabilities as well, such as calculation errors. Software coding is largely about mathematics and calculations; hence the risk of error always exists.

Programmers also sometimes fail to test the boundary conditions of the application. An example of this was the Y2K problem with two digit years 99 and 00. The main problem in software security and overall information security as well, is the huge cost of adding superb security in products and people. In contrast, the cost of completely ignoring security is small. Therefore, the incentives to strengthen the level of information security diminish, while the expenses are high and the benefits are hard to measure.

The organization's connectivity to outer networks also predisposes the organization to vulnerabilities. Typically, an organization has a large amount of entry points, and each of those can be a path for a malicious intruder. A large organization has to efficiently manage its Internet connections.

An organization might have back-door connections to Internet, which is used by test labs or remote access purposes. These other connections might not have the same extent of protection as the main Internet connection, thus they should be considered "outside" networks.

Technical vulnerabilities are a cumbersome issue to the organization's risk environment, since social engineers and malicious insiders can deploy the weaknesses in the technical perimeter, together with human vulnerabilities.

The basics of the threat of economic espionage have not changed significantly in the era of information technology. However, the Internet and information age have re-tooled some espionage techniques. The foundation of the threat is still the same, but the technology has disguised the threat to be broader and faster, as well as more subtle and deceptive. Technology has changed some of the attack vectors and some features of the attacks. Nevertheless, the technology does not attack by itself, since the root of all espionage is always a human, whether it is an insider or outsider. Malicious economic spies are usually motivated by financial greed, and their attacks include deception and hidden actions.

Economic espionage is a serious risk to companies worldwide, and all it takes is one single person or a competitor to endanger a company. The person can be found either inside or outside the company. A common misbelief is that only large corporations are prone to be targets to economic espionage, yet many smaller organizations face the risk as well.

Smaller businesses usually have more competitors than large corporations; therefore, they can be even more exposed to economic espionage. To better illustrate the grave problem of economic espionage, the figures will speak for themselves. According to The International Chamber of Commerce, the estimated fiscal loss from economic espionage was more than $600 billion a year, and according to U.S. Commerce Department, the amount was $250 billion annually, and costing around 750 000 jobs in the United States only.

Due to espionage attacks, corporations all over the world are losing incentives to develop scientific and technological innovations, and this is affecting to the nation's competitive advantage. Trade secret thefts are political issue as well. In the U.S., the gravity of the problem is already affecting the political relations with China, since China is a common culprit in espionage activity towards U.S industrial technology and government's information.

Many companies are concentrating on the physical security by protecting their properties with a lot of effort. Companies are protecting the entrance to the office building, and fencing the 18 surroundings of a warehouse. However, more than 70% of a company's market value comes from intangible assets, such as trade secrets.

To completely understand the depths of economic espionage, companies have to be aware of some details of trade secrets. The most important quality of a trade secret is the secrecy of the information. The owner of a trade secret needs to take a protective approach to the information; otherwise, it is not considered a trade secret at all.

The basic element of the trade secret cannot be generally known to the public, and it cannot be found in public domains. The owner of the secret shall not leak the valuable information to the public by any means, for example in a presentation given to students at a university. Besides being kept as a secret, a trade secret has to contain some element of novelty.

The information regarding to the trade secret cannot be obvious to the competitors, nor can it be generally known to public. However, a trade secret can be a combination of public information and secret information, and the unique combination of information will create a legitimate trade secret.

According to the Economic Espionage Act from 1996, trade secret includes: all forms and types of financial, business, scientific, technical, economic, or engineering information, including patterns, plans, compilations, program devices, formulas, designs, prototypes, methods, techniques, processes, procedures, programs, or codes, whether tangible or intangible, and whether or how stored, compiled, or memorialized physically, electronically, graphically, photographically, or in writing.

The organization that claims to possess the aforementioned trade secret, need to take reasonable measures to control the valuable information and to keep it secure. Therefore, the organization has to educate, train, and advice its employees on regular basis.

Organizations should as well require non-disclosure forms and non-compete clauses, and limit the access of the employees to the trade secrets. In his book (2002), Fink points out that the "open culture" work environment is not the best possible culture regarding to trade secret safety, since the victim of a trade secret theft has to be capable to indicate the occurrence of the crime in a court. In a highly open culture environment, it might be difficult to demonstrate that any security measures were adopted inside the organization.

According to Simon (1998), additionally to the competent security measures, the organization has to be able to prove the independent economic value of the trade secret. Hence, the information should derive economic value, whether actual or potential.

Somewhat confusing concept relating to trade secret thefts is the business intelligence, which is currently an ascending activity among organizations all over the world. This legal activity contains reconnaissance of publicly available information, such as court records, annual reports, government documents, trade fairs, speeches made by executives, and sales reports.

All this is considered open source information, and competitors can legally dwell into these documents. Even though the motives to practice business intelligence are similar to ones of economic espionage, the methods are fundamentally different, since economic espionage is about stealing trade secrets.

Business intelligence only analyzes and scrutinizes useful and legally available information. An example of legal business intelligence is gathering sensitive information in business and scientific seminars, or at international trade shows. Spies from competing companies can act as a potential customer or interested researcher in these open events to obtain valuable information. Competitors can also obtain large amounts of valuable information legally from requested proprietary documents prior to trial.

Legal methods of acquiring trade secrets include the pressuring or "blackmailing" done by actors of foreign country. Some foreign countries, in order to allow foreign companies to do business in their land, are forcing the counterpart to divulge valuable intelligence. This 20 prerequisite of doing business might turn up expensive. Companies might also have to train and employ native workers in a field of critical technology.

Sometimes the only way to enter a foreign market is to assemble a joint venture with a native company. Joint ventures provide great opportunities for the foreign company to tamper sensitive information from the counterpart.

An important part of the business intelligence is reverse engineering, where a company is practicing legal espionage by scrutinizing a competitor's product. The purpose of reverse engineering is to get familiar with the processes and specification in the product's development and manufacture. The company that is practicing reverse engineering, tries to study the item precisely to obtain detailed understanding of the way it works.

The aim is to create similar or even superior products by redesigning the product. The thin line between illegal espionage activities and legal business intelligence is hard to define. As a rule of thumb, anything that can be considered stealing is strictly illegal. Stealing can happen in many subtle ways, which are sometimes hard to prove.

Competitors can recruit a mole from the target company. In such a manner, the company has someone inside the victim organization, working in exchange for money or other benefits. These moles originate from inside and outside, meaning that the malicious company can recruit the insider or the insider can volunteer his or her services as a mole.

Another commonly used method is eavesdropping target employees. This is extremely relative for employees who travel often, since hotel rooms can be eavesdropped or searched during the absence of the guest. Often overlooked because of its simplicity, dumpster diving is another effective way to spy companies.

CONCLUSION

Organizations today have a significant amount of valuable intangible property, which can be considered trade secrets. Other corporations, states, and individuals are interested in those assets, since trade secrets can be easily monetized. Stealing valuable information assets is an ascending crime, and a huge threat to companies of any size, all around the world.

Managing the economic espionage should be addressed more in the risk management literature, since large part of organization's value lies in the proprietary information. Stolen or leaked blueprints of unrevealed products can destroy the whole company, because of the sunken costs in research & development, and the shortfall in revenues.

Business world today is highly dependent on information systems. Large amount of processes are automated, and their vulnerabilities are thought to be technical by nature. In addition, more and more business activities are connected to the Internet, and that is exposing information assets to new kind of risk environment – the cyber world. Information risks consist of confidentiality, integrity, and availability of information.

Organizations try to protect their information assets from diverse threats, such as hackers and system errors. In order to defeat information risks, IT department must design technical security controls, such as firewalls and intrusion detection systems. However, these technical security controls are not sufficient, since human element of information risk is vital regarding to the survivability of the company.

Human element is usually overlooked component of information security, and information risk management as well. As a consequence, the goal of the study was to find suitable and non-technical risk management solutions, which could help organizations to protect their valuable information assets.

To better understand the insider and outsider threats, organizations should understand the connection between the economic espionage attacks and information risks. Trade secret thefts are targeting information by definition, and that particular information lies under the auspices of cyber environment.

These three concepts form a vantage point, through which organizations should evaluate the insider and outsider threats, and plan the risk management solutions. Information risks and economic espionage risks have many similarities and their interconnectivity is evident.

Undoubtedly, information risk is a broader concept, since it considers all the organization's data and operational systems, and the confidentiality, integrity, and availability of information. Economic espionage associates mostly with the confidentiality of the information.

Many information risk attributes, such as cloud computing, have facilitated the execution of trade secret thefts. Internet has completely altered the risk environment of global companies. Malicious competitors and other spying actors are capable of delivering espionage attacks with smaller resources, and from far away from the target.

The peculiar laws of cyber world enable continuous attacks, and foreign perpetrators are enjoying almost complete impunity, since the arm of the international law is powerless in most Internet crimes. Therefore, managing the behavior of organization's employees is an optimal approach to asserting the safety of information confidentiality.

Threats to information assets are diverse, since attacks can derive from various sources. The motivation of an attack usually determines the attack vector.

There are two essential economic espionage threats, which were insider threat and targeted Advanced Persistent Threat (APT). The aforementioned two attack methods are subtle and dangerous, and organizations have difficulties in evaluating, assessing, and alleviating the risks involved. APT attacks cannot be effectively prevented with technical measures, or by any measure whatsoever. Targeted attackers are persistent, and they will generally continue doing the malicious attacks until they penetrate the organization's defense.

Attackers will plan the attacks carefully, and they go to great lengths in defeating the target organization's defense. APT attacks are also well funded, and the sophistication levels of the organizing and planning the attacks indicate precise targeting. Targeted attacks deploy sophisticated malware as well, although the most relevant quality is the human elements of the attack; social engineering and information gathering.

Employees are susceptible to be manipulated, whereas computers work in the way they are programmed. Corporate spies are using the path of least resistance when they attack an organization.

In some cases, technical security controls might be difficult, if not impossible, to circumvent. Therefore, attackers are targeting humans, who are the endpoint of the computer systems. Employees make mistakes, especially when they are constantly under pressure. Malicious attackers have an arsenal of tricks how they can overload the employees' cognitive capabilities, and make the targeted employees to divulge information.

By far, the most common attack method is the traditional phone, and email is a popular method as well. However, phone calls give the targets less time to think the caller's request. Malicious attackers use human related vulnerabilities in accordance with manipulative tricks to build trust between the caller and the target.

Social engineers are well prepared for the attack, since they do a large amount of information gathering prior the attack. Social engineers have a believable pretext that they use in order to elicit valuable information.

Economic spies can either elicit trade secrets directly or gather login and user credentials for later use. Either way, social engineering is an extremely complex but efficient tool for targeted threats.

The goal of analyzing social engineering was to introduce the manifold attack methods, and to delineate the magnitude of the risk for the organization's competitive contingency. Social engineering is not the only attack method of corporate spies. Another stealthy way of spying companies is to use insiders.

There are many types of insiders, with various motivations and goals, and this fact makes it extremely hard for an organization to observe malicious or threatening activity. Organizations must find a balance between healthy skepticism and paranoia. Companies should not start persecuting or victimizing employees without airtight evidence. Nevertheless, any suspicious activity should be taken seriously.

Diminished loyalty towards an employer has caused dissatisfaction at workplaces. Employers should observe at least two aspects regarding to insider threats. First thing is the motivation to commit trade secret thefts, since employees have various problems that lead to desperate solutions. Secondly, employers should control the situations, where employees have convenient opportunity to steal valuable data assets.

The assessment of the insider risk is important for managers, since they must recognize the threat, and the consequences of the realized risk. Malicious insider activities are more commonplace problems of large economic superpowers, such as in the U.S. and Germany.

However, insider attacks occur in Finland as well. An efficient natural obstacle for social engineers in Finland is the complex language, which complicates the attacking methods. However, many multinational companies in Finland use English as official working language; hence, social engineers can approach the targets without translators.

In the case of economic espionage, companies usually do not have any recourse to the law. Therefore, companies must seek other remedies to battle against the insider and outsider threats. One of the biggest impediments of information security is that a separate technical department is controlling the information risks.

Organizations should facilitate the communication between IT personnel and other managers, and all decisions should align with the organization's overall risk management strategy. Enterprise Risk Management (ERM) is an optimal tool for this. The goal of the ERM is to align all departments together, in order to provide harmonized risk analysis for the board.

IT security has its own peculiarities, since it contains technical jargon that is incomprehensible to other managers. In order to mitigate economic espionage, some important issues should be considered in the operational and strategic risk management procedures.

These important issues are data classification, awareness of the threats, policies and guidelines, and penetration testing. With a profound research of literature, these areas were the most convenient and effective risk management controls against social engineering and insider threats.

All employees should know the reasons why each classified data asset is protected. Mere authentication policies are not sufficient, if employees do not fathom the reasoning behind it. Employees make security tradeoffs if the security measures cause inconvenience.

The situation could be different if employees knew the rationale behind the compulsory security measures. Each valuable information asset that is susceptible to economic espionage should have an owner, custodian, and user. This classification technique clarifies the reporting and documenting roles of each classified data.

Threat awareness is a closely related subject to data classification. By raising awareness, it is possible to steer the employees' behavior. Data classification considers why valuable data is in need of protection, while threat awareness is about recognizing the attacks and knowing the motivations behind the attacks

Social engineering is a collection of deceptive tools, and organization's employees have to be aware of those tricks, and how attackers can approach target employees with malicious incentives. En example of effective risk management solution is to go through social engineering cases.

This is a practical way to enhance the awareness of the risk. From the case based learning, employees could observe how social engineers can elicit pieces of mundane information, and how the attackers are using the mundane information to approach other employees.

Employees should be taught to respond correctly to weird requests, and through awareness training, organizations should demonstrate the manifold ways social engineers might approach the organization's employees. Awareness training should be systematic and dynamic. Each employee should participate in the training, and the trainings should be repeated at certain intervals. The most concrete way to direct the behavior of organization's employees is to add strict and precise policies, which will guide the employee's actions in abnormal situations.

Policy implementing and awareness training should go hand in hand, since they are pretty much useless without the other. Policies have no function if employees do not obey them or understand them. Vice versa, awareness training is a waste of time if organization is not guiding the behavior with strict rules. Neglecting the policies will lead to an organizational culture of neglect.

Therefore, policy development should be a well-planned process, where various departments should collaborate. One big mistake is to assess the policies in total isolation from risk management strategy and data classification processes. It is also crucial to remember that organizational habits can sometimes be deeply embedded in the organizational culture, and they are not easily changed.

Policies and guidelines should be evaluated continuously, since the attack methods and attack vectors are changing all the time. This is due to the inconsistent nature of information risk environment, where short technical development circles change the risks constantly. However, steering the behavior of employees with policies is not a panacea in thwarting trade secret thefts.

The final risk management solution is to test the organization's human vulnerabilities. Vulnerability is a flaw or weakness in the asset's defense, and the objective of penetration testing is to strengthen the asset's defense. Penetration testing is a critical risk management phase, since it is giving immediate feedback from the organization's defense and risk controls.

REFERENCES

1. AGREEMENT ON TRADE-RELATED ASPECTS OF INTELLECTUAL PROPERTY RIGHTS (1994).
2. Albrecht Glitz and Erik Meyersson (JUNE 2017). Industrial Espionage and Productivity, Discussion Paper Series, IZA DP No. 10816.
3. Almeling, D. S. (2009). Four Reasons to Enact a Federal Trade Secrets. *Fordham Intellectual Property, Media and Entertainment Law Journal, 19*(3). Retrieved from http://law.fordham.edu/publications/
4. Almeling, D. S. (2012). Seven Reasons Why Trade Secrets Are Increasingly Important. *Berkeley Tech. L.J., 27.* doi:http://dx.doi.org/doi:10.15779/Z38SM4F
5. Alperovitch, D. (2011). *Revealed: Operation Shady RAT, An investigation of targeted intrusions into more than 70 global companies, governments,and non-profit organizations during the last five years.* McAfee.
6. American Bar Association. (2010, July/August). Trade Secrets v. Patents: The New Calculus by R. Mark Halligan. *Landslide volume 2, number 6*, p. 3.
7. Ankenbrandt, B., & Vormann, T. (2016). *Comparing U.S. and EU Trade Secret Laws.* Trans-Atlantic Business Council, Intellectual Property Working Group. Retrieved from www.transatlanticbusiness.org
8. Aplin, T. (2014). *A Critical Evaluation of the Proposed EU Trade Secrets Directive.* King's College London, Dickson Poon School of Law.
9. Beckerman-Rodau, A. (2002). The Choice between Patent Protection and Trade Secret Protection: A legal and Business Decision.
10. Bevitt, A., Timner, H., & Westerman, D. (2014, June). Protecting Trade Secrets Globally: Compating The U.S. and EU. *Employment Law Commentary, 26.* Retrieved from http://www.mofo.com/~/media/Files/Newsletter/140630EmploymentLawCommentary.pdf
11. Bone, R. G. (1998). A New Look at Trade Secret Law: Doctrine in Search for Justification. *California Law Review, 86*(2). doi:http://dx.doi.org/doi:10.15779/Z38942G

12. Boulay, C. (2015). *QUESTION B The Protection of Trade Secrets and Know-How Are countries providing enough or too much protection?* University of Neuchâtel, Center for Intellectual Property and Innovation Law.
13. Center for Responsible Enterprise and Trade. (2014). Safeguarding Trade Secrets and Mitigating Threats: A Five-Step Framework to Identify, Assess and Manage Trade Secrets. Elements of an Effective Trade Secret Protection Program. CREATe.org, PwC. Retrieved from www.CREATe.org
14. Center for Responsible Enterprise and Trade. (2015). *"Reasonable Steps" to protect Trade Secrets: Leading Practices in an Evolving Legal Landscape.* Retrieved from www.CREATe.org. 55
15. Congress, S. a. (2016, May 11). To amend chapter 90 of title 18, United States Code, to provide Federal jurisdiction for the theft of trade secrets, and for other purposes."Defend Trade Secrets Act of 2016". Retrieved from https://www.congress.gov/bill/114th-congress/senate-bill/1890/text
16. Crouch, D. (2016, January 18). Guest Post: Why we Need a Seizure Remedy in the Defend Trade Secrets Act. *Patentlyo*. Retrieved from http://patentlyo.com/patent/2016/01/seizure-secrets-dtsa.html
17. Dass, N., Nanda, V., & Chong Xiao, S. (2014, October). Intellectual Property Protection and Financial Markets: Patenting vs. Secrecy. Retrieved from www2.warwick.ac.uk/fac/soc/wbs/subjects/finance/events/.../innoprotect_v4b.pdf
18. DIRECTIVE OF THE EUROPEAN PARLIAMENT AND OF THE COUNCIL on the protection of undisclosed know-how and business information (trade secrets) against their unlawful acquisition, use and disclosure. (2016, April 26). THE EUROPEAN PARLIAMENT AND THE COUNCIL OF THE EUROPEAN UNION. Retrieved from http://eur-lex.europa.eu/legal-content/EN/TXT/PDF/?uri=CELEX:32016L0943&from=EN
19. Engel Industries, Inc. v. The Lockformer Company, No.95-1185 (United States Court of Appeals, Federal Circuit September 25, 1996).
20. European Commission. (2013). *Impact Assessment on a proposal for a Directive of the European Parliament and of*

the Council on the protection of undisclosed know-how and business information (trade secrets) against misappropriation. Commission Staff Working Document, Brussels. Retrieved from http://eur-lex.europa.eu/legal-content/EN/TXT/?uri=CELEX%3A52013SC0471

21. European Parliament News. (2015, June 16). Trade Secrets: freedom of expression must be protected, say legal affairs MEPs.
22. Executive Office of the President of the United States. (2013). *ADMINISTRATION STRATEGY ON MITIGATING THE THEFT OF U.S. TRADE SECRETS.* Retrieved from https://www.whitehouse.gov/sites/default/files/omb/IPEC/admin_strategy_on_mitigating_the_theft_of_u.s._trade_secrets.pdf
23. Final Study, April 2013, Study on Trade Secrets and Confidential Business Information in the Internal Market Prepared for the European Commission, Contract number: MARKT/2011/128/D.
24. Forrester Consulting. (2012). *The Value of Corporate Secrets, How Compliance and Collaboration Affects Enterprise Perception of Risk.* Retrieved from www.forrester.com
25. General Intelligence and Security Service, Ministry of the Interior and Kingdom Relations. (2014). *ANNUAL REPORT AIVD.* Retrieved from www.aivd.nl
26. Goldam, E., Levine, D. S., Sandeen, S. K., Seaman, C. B., Bambauer, J., Bessen, J., . . . Wiant, S. K. (2015, November 17). Professors' Letter in Opposition to the Defend Trade Secret Act of 2015. Retrieved from https://cyberlaw.stanford.edu/files/blogs/2015%20Professors%20Letter%20in%20Opposition%20to%20DTSA%20FINAL.pdf
27. Goldman, E. (2015). Ex Parte Seizures and the Defend Trade Secrets Act. *Washington and Lee Law Review Online, 72*(2). Retrieved from http://scholarlycommons.law.wlu.edu/wlulr-online/vol72/iss2/4 56
28. Halligan, R. M. (2015). Revisited 2015: Protection of U.S. Trade Secret Assets: Critical Amendments to the Economic Espionage Act of 1996. *MARSHALL REV. INTELL. PROP. L.*
29. International Chamber of Commerce. (2014). Trade Secrets: Tools for Innovation and Collaboration. p.9.

30. James H.A. Pooleya, Mark A. Lemleyaa and Peter J. Torenaaa, Understanding The Economic Espionage Act Of 1996, Texas Intellectual Property Law Journal, Winter, 1997.
31. Jorgenson, D. W., & Vu, K. M. (2016, February 5). The ICT revolution, world economic growth and policy issues. *ELSERVIER*, 383-397. doi:10.1016/j.telpol.2016.01.002
32. Klitzke, R. A. (1980). The Uniform Trade Secret Act. *Marquette Law Review, 64*(2). Retrieved from http://scholarship.law.marquette.edu/mulr/vol64/iss2/2
33. Knaak, R., Kur, A., & Hilty, R. M. (2014, June 3). Comments of the Max Planck Institute for Innovation and Competition . Retrieved from http://ssrn.com/abstract=2464971
34. Lahodynsky, O. (2015, June 15). EU trade bill threatens media freedom. *eurobserver*.
35. Linton, K. (2016, March). The Unexpected Importance of Trade Secrets: New Directions in International Trade Policy Making and Empirical Research.
36. Lippoldt, D. C., & Schultz., M. F. (2014). Trade Secrets, Innovation and the WTO. Geneva, Switzerland: International Center for Trade and Sustainable Development (ICTSD) and World Economic Forum. Retrieved from www.e15initiave.org/
37. Meltzer, J. (2013, February). The Internet, Cross-border Data Flows and International Trade. *Issues in Technology Innovation (22)*. Center for Technology Innovation at Brookings. Retrieved from https://www.brookings.edu/research/the-internet-cross-border-data-flows-and-international-trade/
38. Nair, M. (2002, August 27). Protection of Trade Secrets/Undisclosed Information. *Journal of Intellectual Property Rights, 7*, 527.
39. Osman David Mejia Hernandez,Trade Secret Protection In The U.S. And Eu, Supervisor: Prof. Mr. E.P. M. Vermeulen, Tilburg, The Netherlands, AUGUST 23, 2016.
40. Pellegrino, M. (2015, June 5). The Threat of State-Sponsored Industrial Espionage. *European Union Institute for Security Studies*(26). Retrieved from http://www.iss.europa.eu/publications/detail/article/the-threat-of-state-sponsored-industrial-espionage/
41. Pooley, J. (2013, June). Trade Secrets: The Other IP Right. *WIPO Magazine*. Retrieved from

http://www.wipo.int/wipo_magazine/en/2013/03/article_0001.html

42. Quinn Emanuel Urquhart and Sullivan LLP. (2012, April 2). Spotlight on the Economic Espionage Act. *Lexology*. Retrieved from http://www.lexology.com/library/detail.aspx?g=d7ac3398-5ff9-44ca-ba44-03bc6cd1eb16

43. Samuelson, P. (2002). *Reverse Engineering Under Seige*. Available at: http://scholarship.law.berkeley.edu/facpubs/2383.

44. Schultz, M. F., & Lippoldt, D. C. (2014). *APPROACHES TO PROTECTION OF UNDISCLOSED INFORMATION (TRADE SECRETS) - BACKGROUND PAPER*. Organisation for Economic Co-operation and Development (OECD). Retrieved from http://www.oecd.org/trade 57

45. Senate and House of Representatives of the United States of America in Congress assembled. (1996, October 11). PUBLIC LAW 104 - 294 - ECONOMIC ESPIONAGE ACT OF 1996. *An act to amend title 18, United States Code, to protect proprietary economic information, and for other purposes.* Retrieved from https://www.gpo.gov/fdsys/pkg/PLAW-104publ294/content-detail.html

46. Sinclair v. Aquarius Electronics, Inc., Civ.No.31700 (Court of Appeals of California, First Appellate District, Division Two October 2, 1974).

47. Spencer, S. (1998). The Economic Espionage Act of 1996. *Berkeley Tech. L.J.* 305. doi:http://dx.doi.org/doi:10.15779/Z38X95T

48. The Commission on the Theft of American Intellectual Property. (2013). *The Report of the Commission on the Theft of American Intellectual Property*. The National Bureau of Asian Research. Retrieved from http://www.ipcommission.org/

49. The Office of the United States Trade Representative. (2015). *2015 Special 301 Report*. Retrieved from https://ustr.gov/sites/default/files/2015-Special-301-Report-FINAL.pdf

50. The University of Melbourne, Melbourne Institute of Applied Economics and Social Research. (2004). On the Interaction between Patent Policy and Trade Secret Policy.

51. UNIFORM TRADE SECRETS ACT WITH 1985 AMENDMENTS. (1985). NATIONAL CONFERENCE OF COMMISSIONERS ON UNIFORM STATE LAWS. Retrieved from http://www.uniformlaws.org/Search.aspx?cx=014921086760789645719:at7aeght8rg&cof=FORID%3A9&ie=UTF-8&q=uniform%20trade%20secret%20act&sa=Search
52. United States International Trade Commission. (2011). *China: Effects of IP Infringement and Indigenous Innovation Policies on the U.S. Economy.* Retrieved from http://www.usitc.gov
53. United States of America, Plaintiff-Appelle, v. Joya Williams, Defendant- Appellant, 07-12526, 07-12653 (United States Court of Appeals, Eleventh Circuit March 20, 2008).
54. Villasenor, J. (2015, August). Corporate CyberSecurity Realism: Managing Trade Secrets in a World Where Breaches Occur. *Quarterly Journal, 43.*
55. W. Kintner, E., & L. Lahr, J. (1975). *An Intellectual Property Law Primer* . New York: Macmillan Publishing Co., Inc.; Collier Macmillian Publishers.
56. Yeh, B. T. (2016, April 22). Protection of Trade Secrets:Overview of Current Law and Legislation. *Congressional Research Service.* Retrieved from https://www.fas.org/sgp/crs/secrecy/R43714.pdf

www.ingramcontent.com/pod-product-compliance
Lightning Source LLC
Chambersburg PA
CBHW031419210526
45464CB00005B/1965